1960s

Ten Years of Popular Hits Arranged for **EASY PIANO**

Arranged by Dan Coates

Contents

AL DI LA

In 1956 the European Broadcasting Union created the *Eurovision Song Contest* to reunite a war-torn Europe. The internationally televised show was an enormous success and will celebrate its 58th anniversary in 2008. "Al di là" was the official Italian entry in 1961, performed by Betty Curtis.

English Words by Ervin Drake
Original Italian Words by Mogol

Music by C. Donida
Arranged by Dan Coates

5

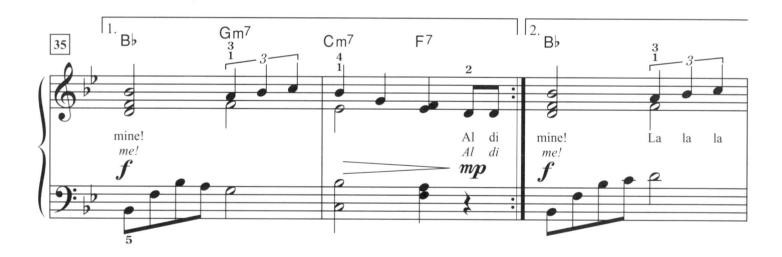

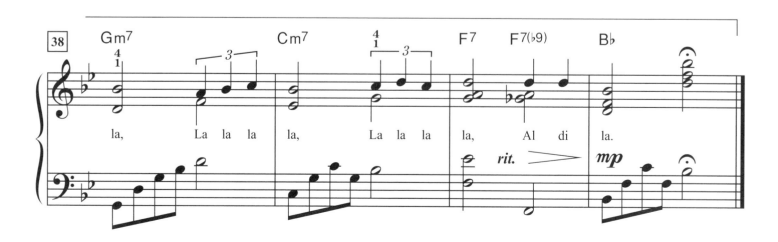

THE BALLAD OF GILLIGAN'S ISLE

CBS aired the hit sitcom *Gilligan's Island* between 1964 and 1967. The premise involved seven people of various social positions—a millionaire and his wife, a movie star, a professor, a farm girl, a ship captain and his first mate—shipwrecked on an uninhabited island somewhere in the middle of the Pacific Ocean. The title character has become one of America's top pop icons.

Words and Music by
Sherwood Schwartz and George Wyle
Arranged by Dan Coates

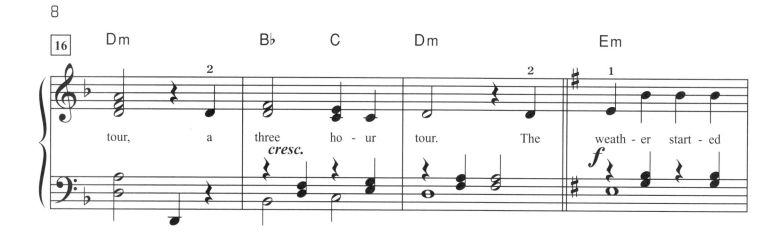

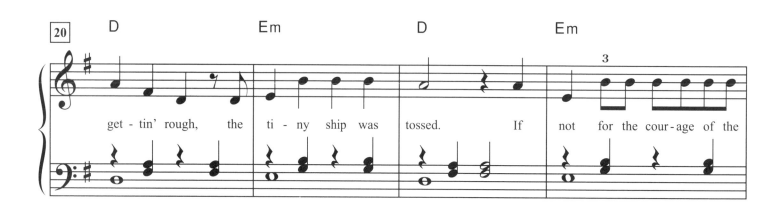

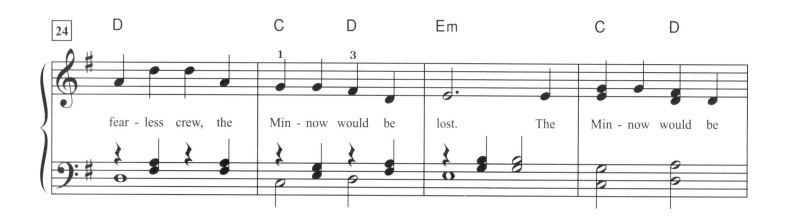

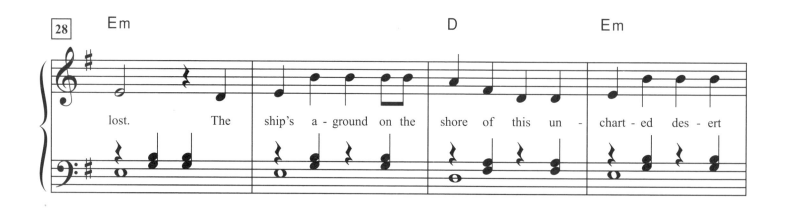

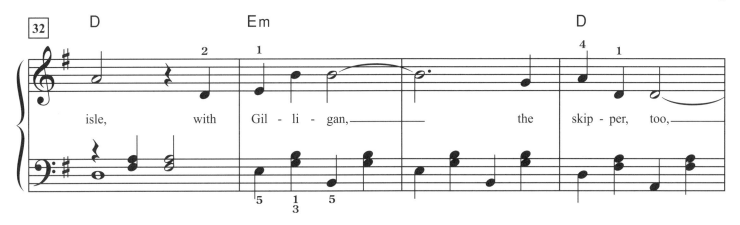

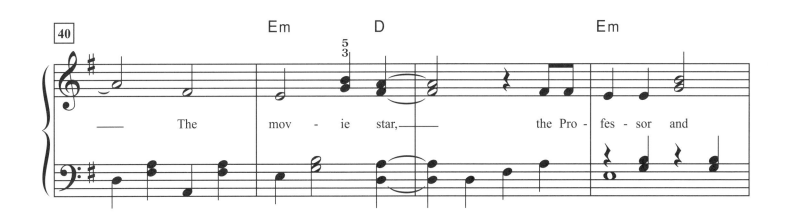

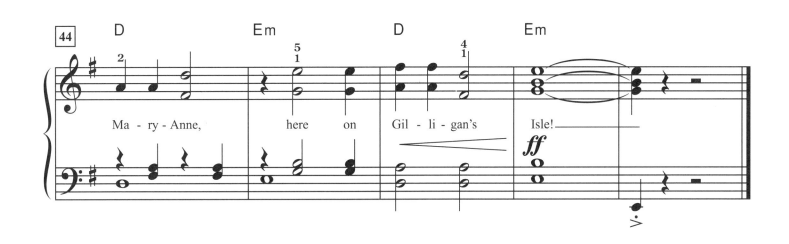

AQUARIUS

"Aquarius" originated in the 1969 musical *Hair*, a revolutionary work which defined the "rock musical" genre and ran for thousands of performances on Broadway and in London. The Fifth Dimension released a medley of "Aquarius" and "Let the Sunshine In" (one of the numbers from the second act) in 1969. It held the #1 position on the Billboard Hot 100 chart for six weeks and went platinum.

Music by Galt MacDermot
Words by James Rado and Gerome Ragni
Arranged by Dan Coates

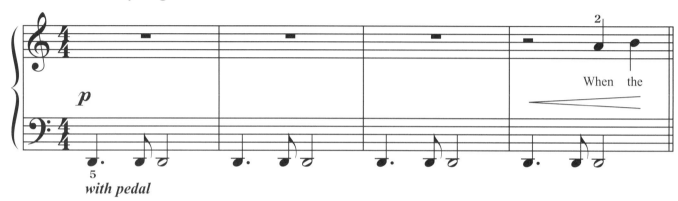

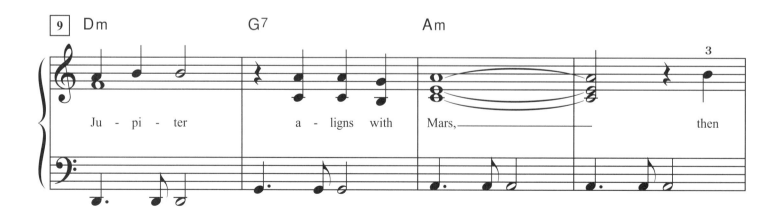

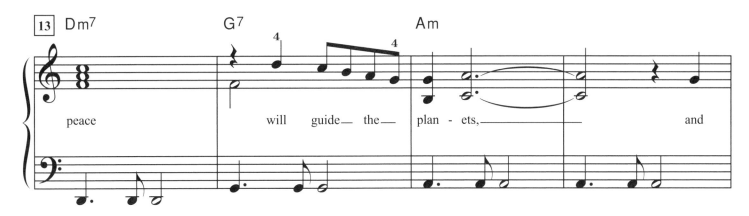

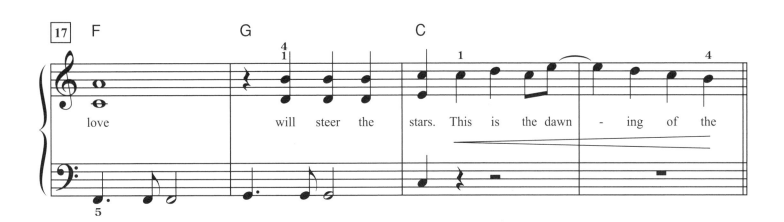

Chorus:

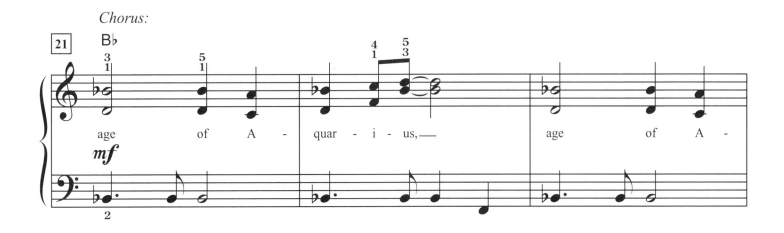

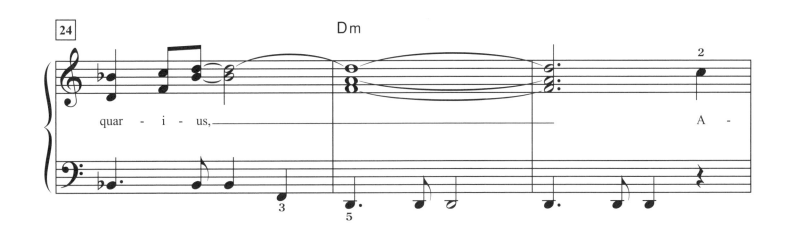

12

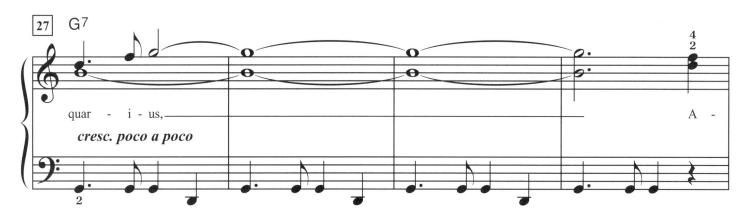

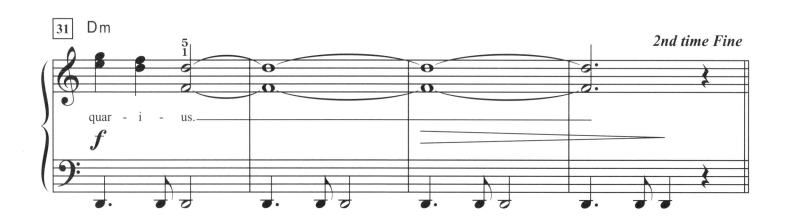

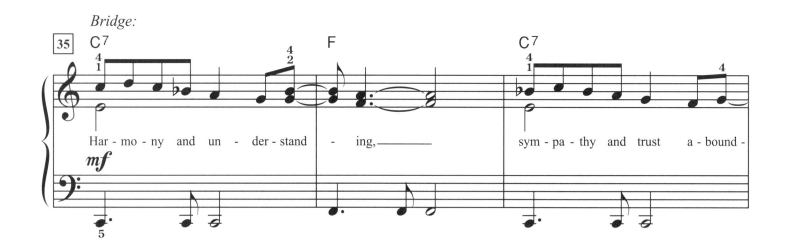

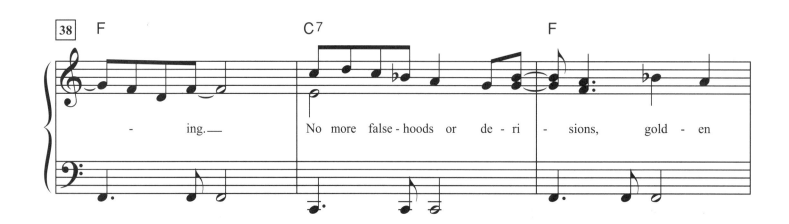

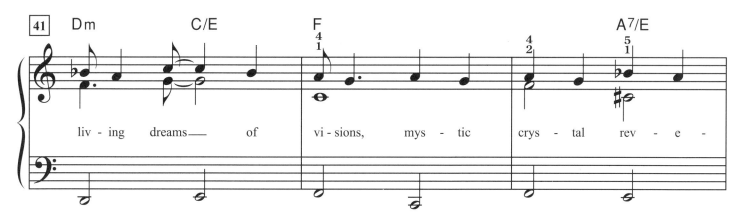

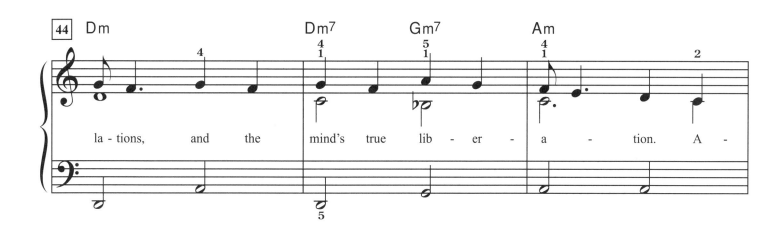

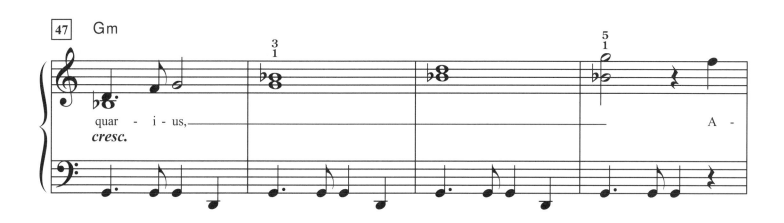

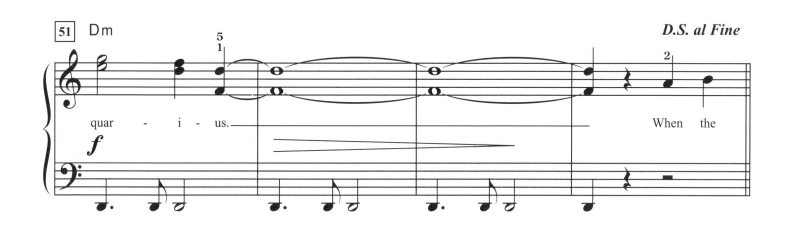

BATMAN THEME

With three chords and a one-word lyric, the music for the *Batman* television series has become one of the best-known themes of all time. It was the most recorded song of 1966. The TV show itself waned in popularity by its third season, but will be remembered as one of the great camp classics of the '60s.

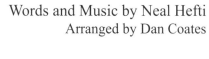

Words and Music by Neal Hefti
Arranged by Dan Coates

With a steady, driving beat

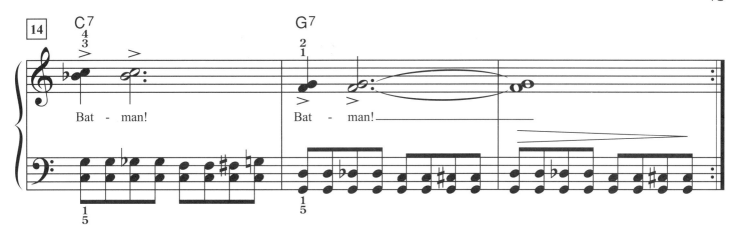

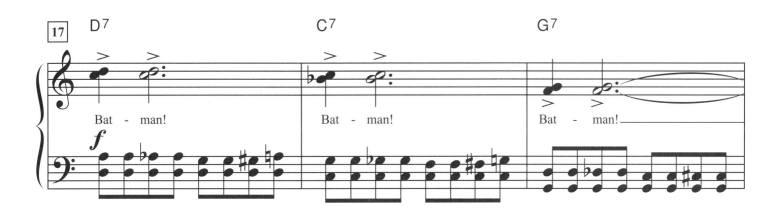

BUILD ME UP BUTTERCUP

The Foundations were a diverse British soul band—whose members came from the West Indies, Sri Lanka and London—and were active in the late-'60s. They are most famous for their chart-topping "Baby, Now That I've Found You" (1967) and "Build Me Up Buttercup" (1968). The latter found its way into two popular movies in the '90s: *Mallrats* and *There's Something About Mary.*

Words and Music by
Tony Macaulay and Michael d'Abo
Arranged by Dan Coates

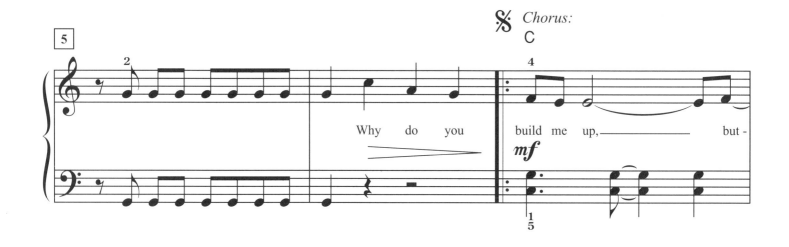

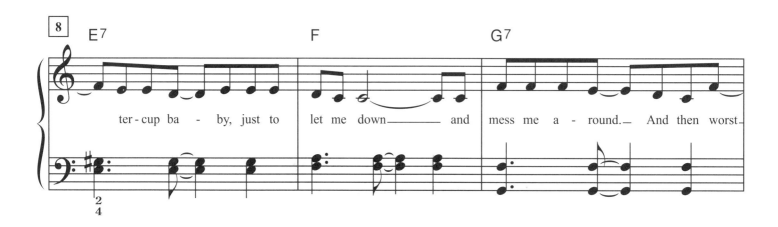

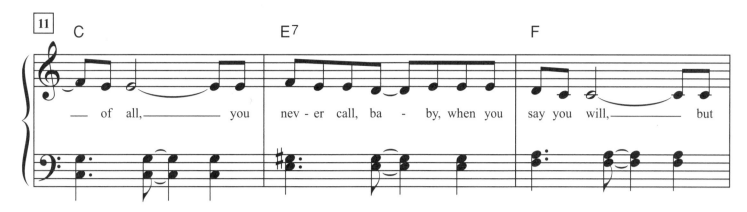

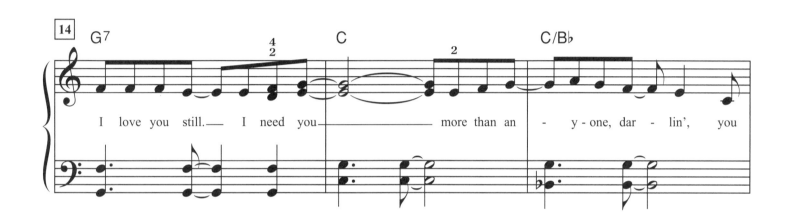

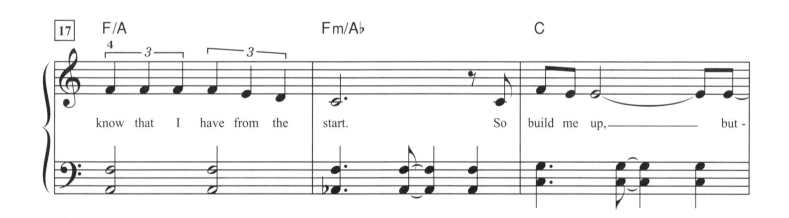

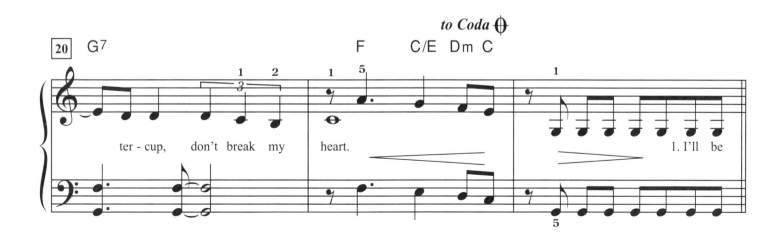

18

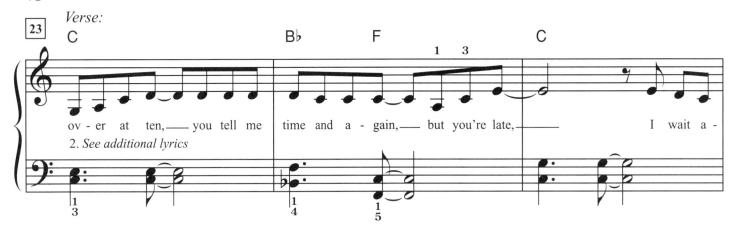

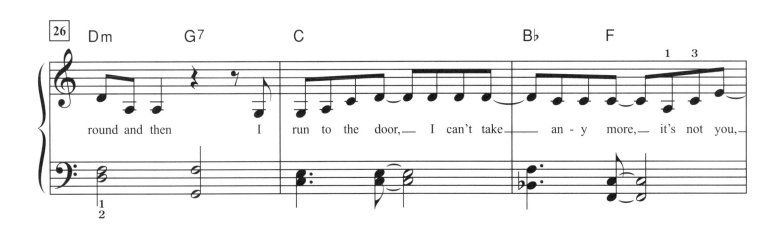

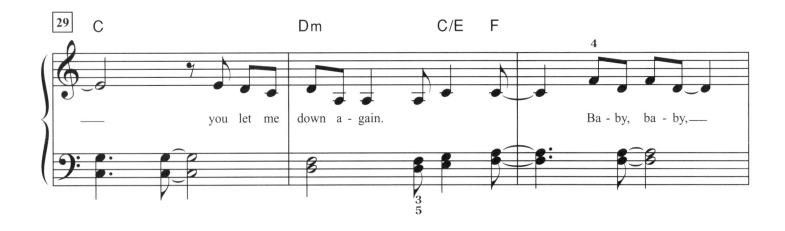

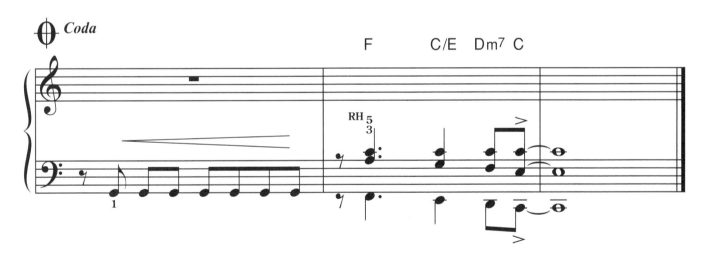

Verse 2:
To you I'm a toy
But I could be the boy you adore,
If you just let me know.
And though you're untrue
I'm attracted to you all the more.
Why do I need you so?
Baby, baby
Try to find
A little time
And I'll make you happy,
I'll be home,
I'll be beside the phone,
Waiting for you.
Oo, Oo.
(To Chorus:)

THE DAYS OF WINE AND ROSES

Blake Edwards directed Jack Lemmon and Lee Remick in the 1962 Academy Award-winning film *Days of Wine and Roses*, a story about a couple that faces alcoholism. The Best Original Song was written by Henry Mancini with lyrics by Johnny Mercer. The phrase "days of wine and roses" is originally from a poem by a late-19th century English poet, Ernest Dowson.

Lyric by Johnny Mercer
Music by Henry Mancini
Arranged by Dan Coates

DON'T RAIN ON MY PARADE

If "People" (on page 96) is the great ballad from *Funny Girl*, "Don't Rain on My Parade" is *Funny Girl's* great up-tempo number. Barbra Streisand sang it both in the original Broadway production (1964) and in the film adaptation (1968). It is a particularly challenging song to sing with its fast, consonant-heavy lyrics in the verses, and with its huge, climactic, belty ending.

Music by Jule Styne
Words by Bob Merrill
Arranged by Dan Coates

Brightly, with a steady beat

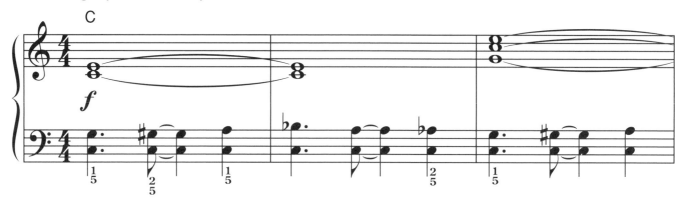

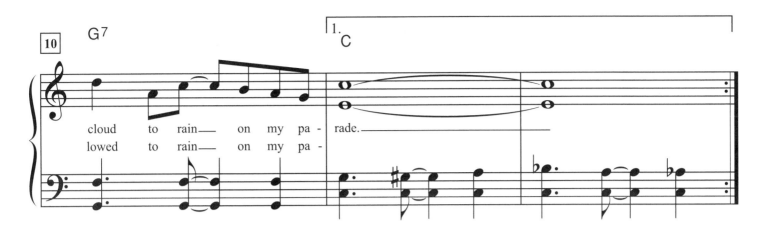

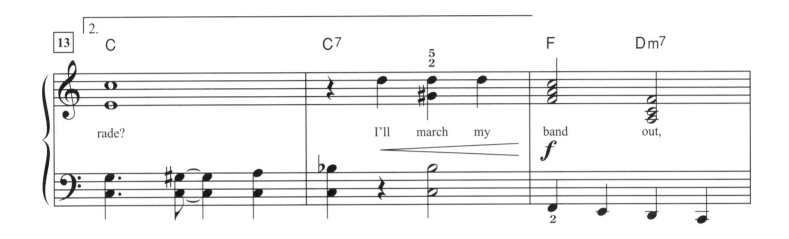

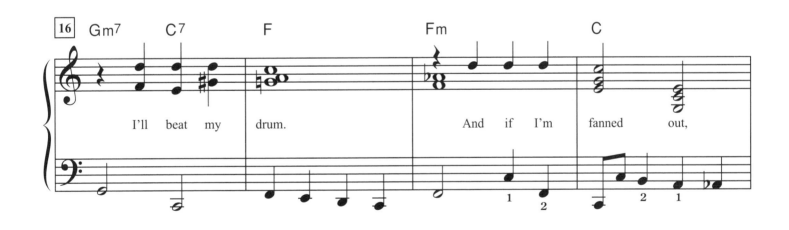

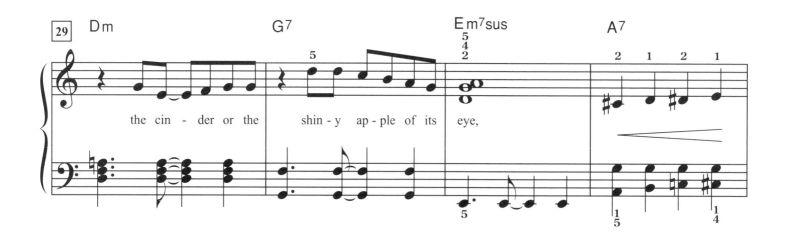

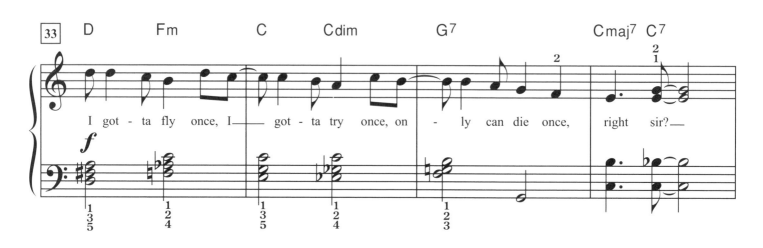

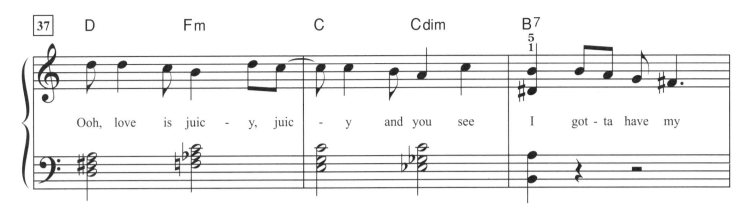

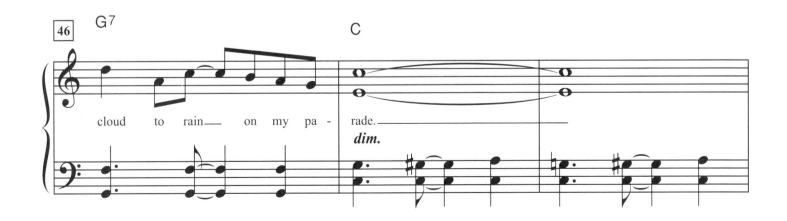

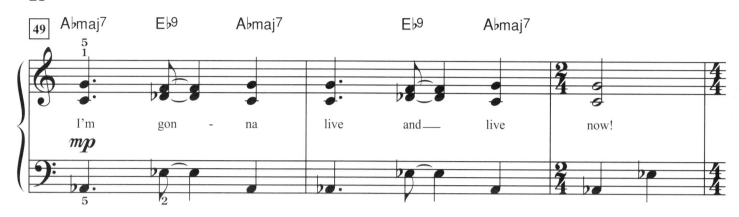

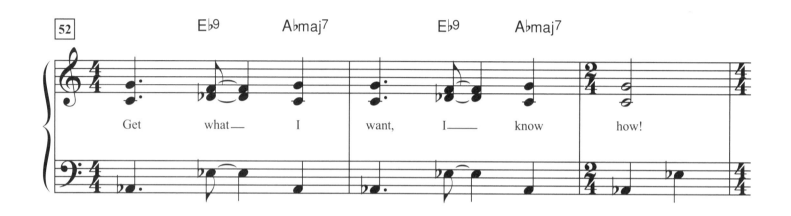

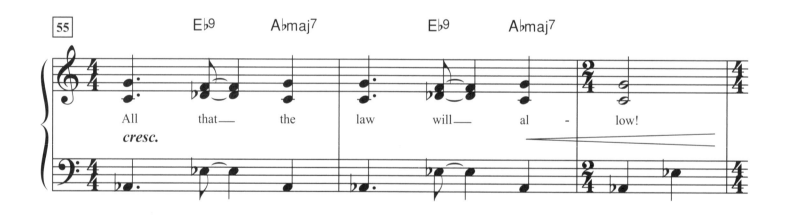

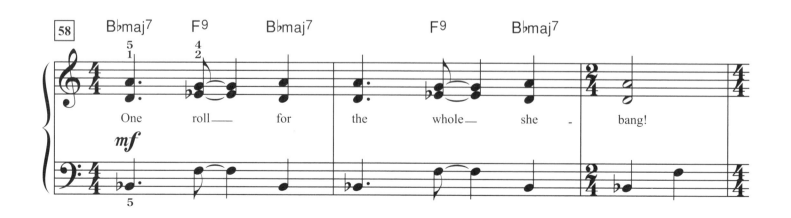

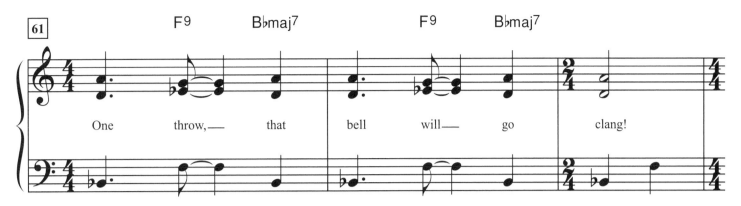

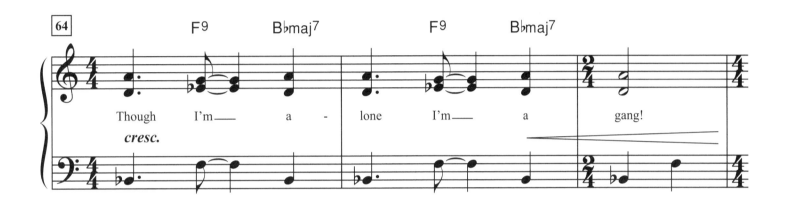

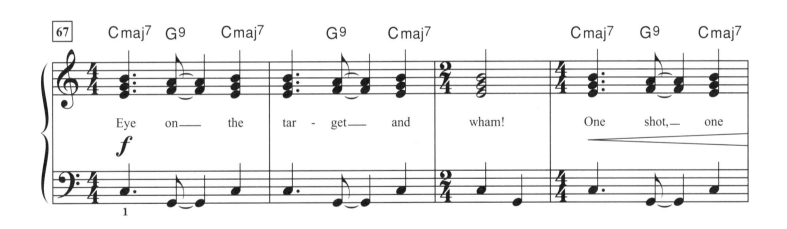

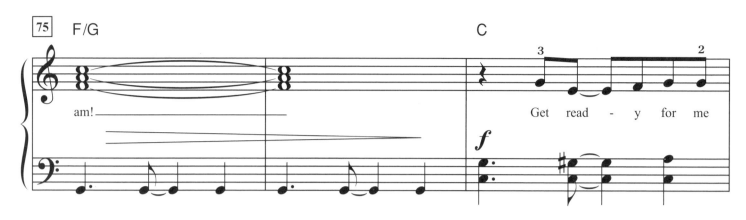

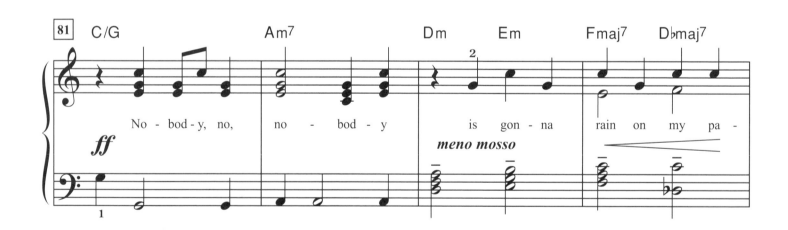

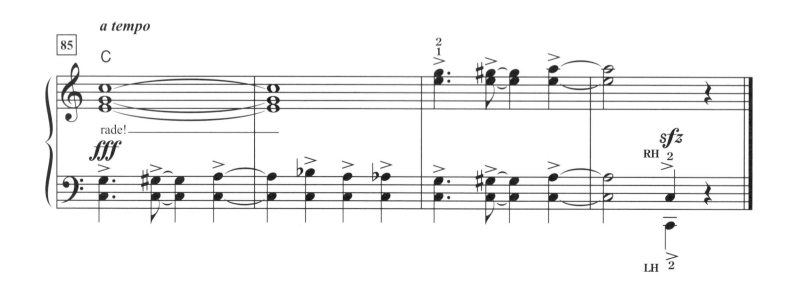

DO YOU WANT TO KNOW A SECRET?

John Lennon and Paul McCartney co-wrote "Do You Want to Know a Secret?" for George Harrison to sing on the Beatles 1963 album *Please Please Me*. It was released as a single in 1964 and reached #2 on the charts behind another Beatles song, "Can't Buy Me Love."

Words and Music by
John Lennon and Paul McCartney
Arranged by Dan Coates

You'll nev - er know how much I real - ly love you,

you'll nev - er know how much I real - ly care.

Lis - ten, do you want to know a sec - ret?

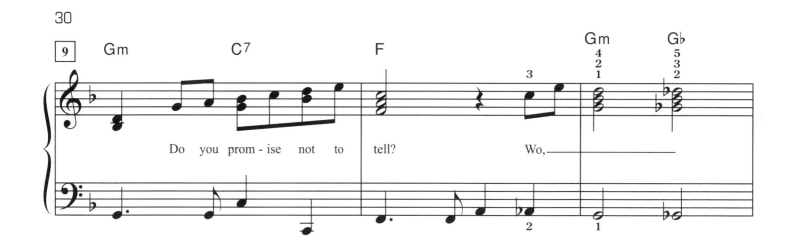

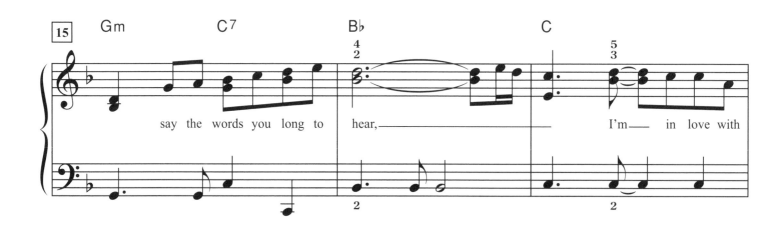

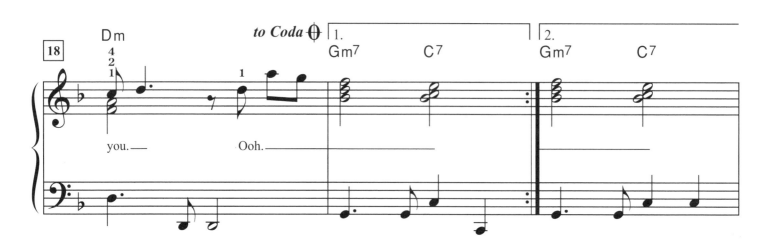

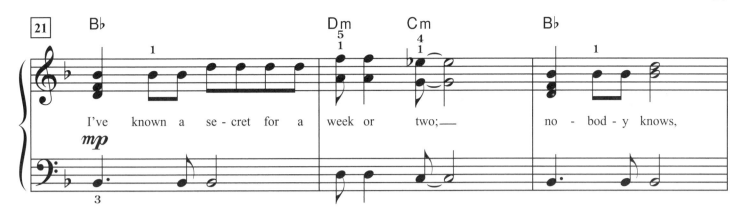

I've known a se-cret for a week or two; — no-bod-y knows,

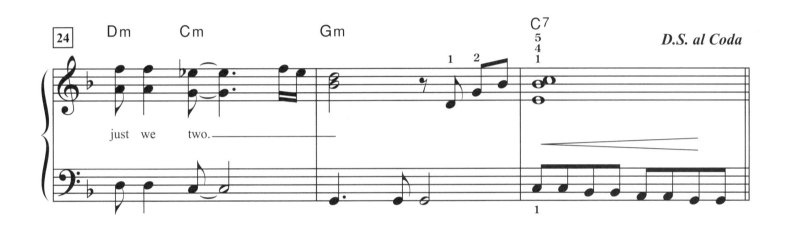

just we two. — *D.S. al Coda*

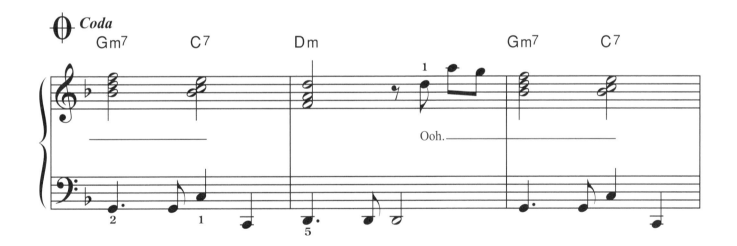

Ooh. —

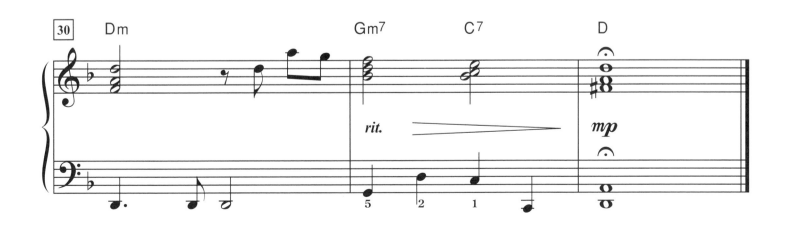

GEORGY GIRL

"Georgy Girl" is the title song from the 1966 British film of the same name. The movie was nominated for two Academy Awards: Best Original Song (as performed by The Seekers, an Australian band) and Best Actress (Lynn Redgrave in the title role). The song reached the top of the charts in the U.S., Australia, and Great Britain.

Words and Music by
Jim Dale and Tom Springfield
Arranged by Dan Coates

Hey there!— Geor-gy girl,— swing-ing down the street so fan-cy free,

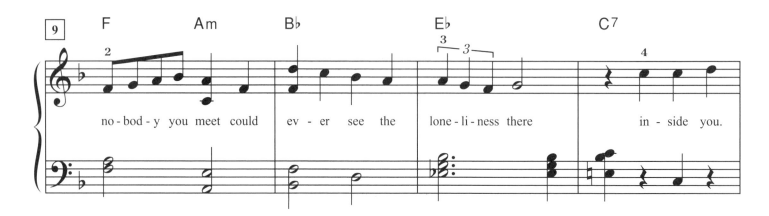

no-bod-y you meet could ev-er see the lone-li-ness there in-side you.

13
| F | Am | Bb | C | F | Am | Gm7 | C7 |

{ 1. Hey there!— Geor-gy girl,— why do all the boys just pass you by?
{ 2. Hey there!— Geor-gy girl,— dream-ing of the some-one you could be.

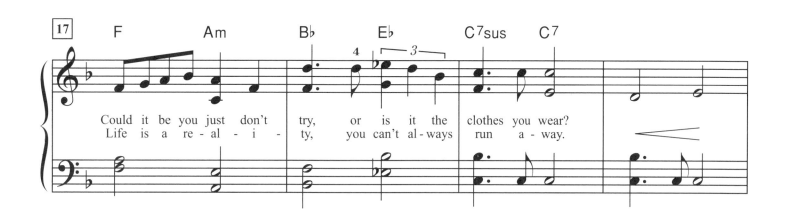

17
| F | Am | Bb | Eb | C7sus | C7 |

Could it be you just don't try, or is it the clothes you wear?
Life is a re-al-i-ty, you can't al-ways run a-way.

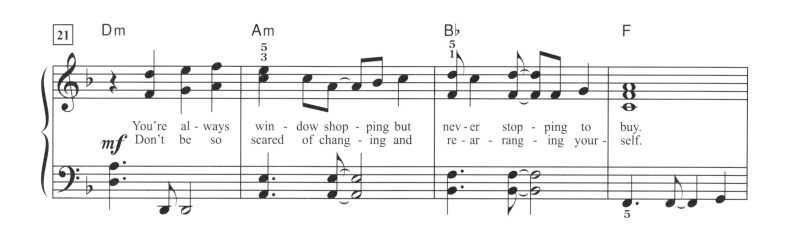

21
| Dm | Am | Bb | F |

mf

You're al-ways win-dow shop-ping but nev-er stop-ping to buy.
Don't be so scared of chang-ing and re-ar-rang-ing your-self.

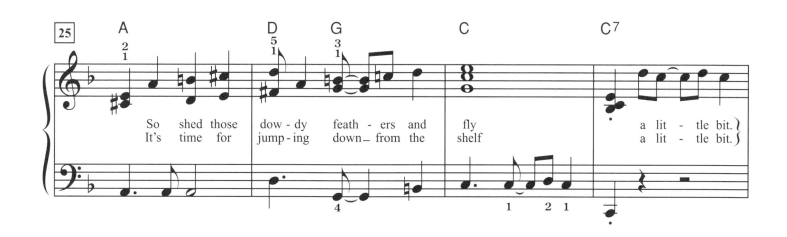

25
| A | D | G | C | C7 |

So shed those dow-dy feath-ers and fly a lit-tle bit. }
It's time for jump-ing down— from the shelf a lit-tle bit. }

34

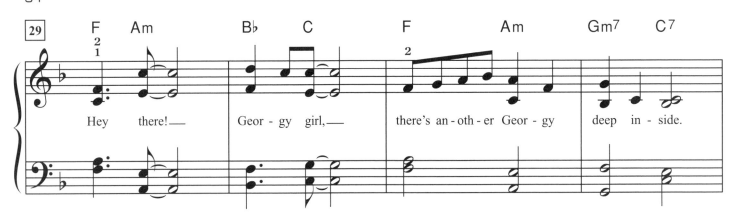

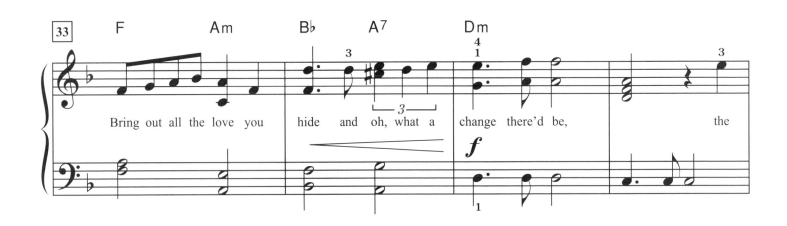

THE GOOD LIFE

"The Good Life" was published in 1962 and was most notably recorded by Tony Bennett in 1963. It became a staple song for Bennett. He named his 1998 autobiography after the song, and he also recorded it as a duet with Billy Joel on his 2006 album *Duets: An American Classic*.

Words by Jack Reardon
Music by Sacha Distel
Arranged by Dan Coates

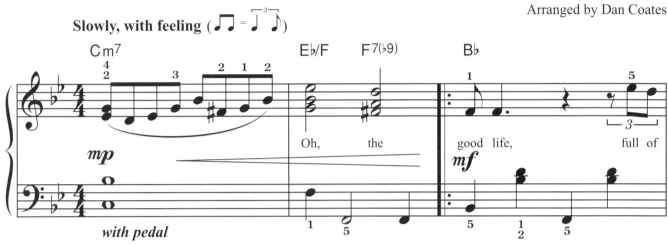

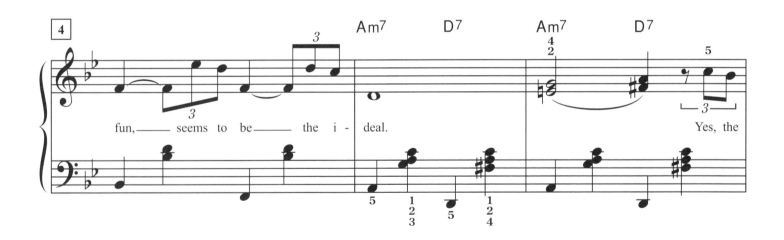

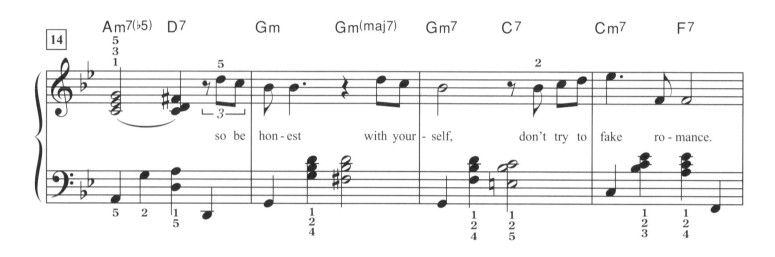

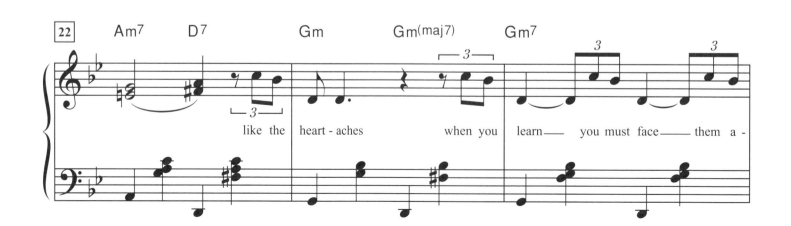

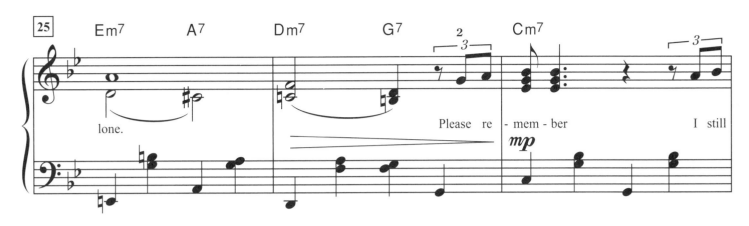

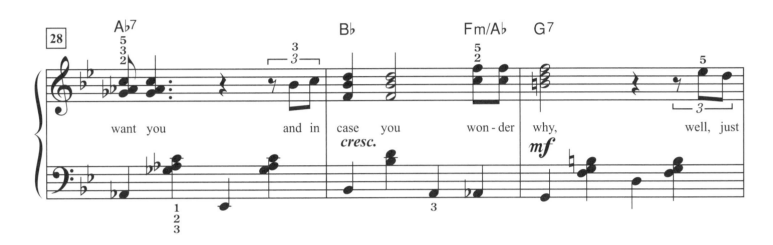

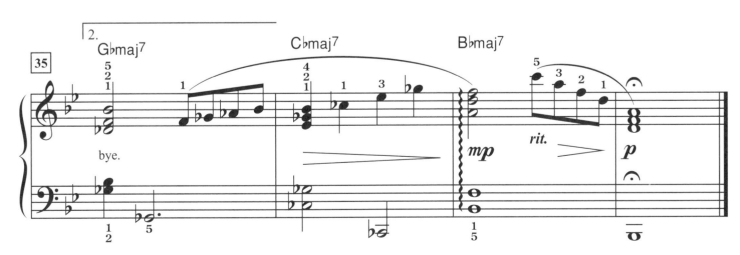

GIMME SOME LOVIN'

At 19 years of age, Steve Winwood came out with "Gimme Some Lovin'." The year was 1967, and he was lead singer of the Spencer Davis Group. Since then the song has been covered by many artists, perhaps most famously by Dan Aykroyd and John Belushi in the 1980 film *The Blues Brothers*.

Words and Music by
Steve Winwood, Muff Winwood and Spencer Davis
Arranged by Dan Coates

Moderately, with a steady beat

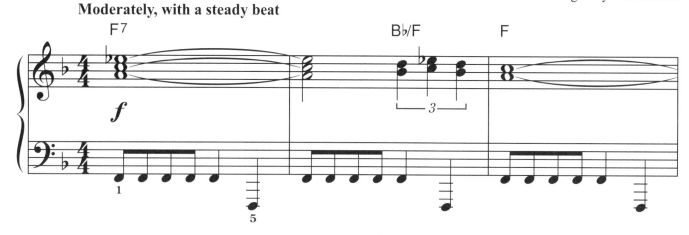

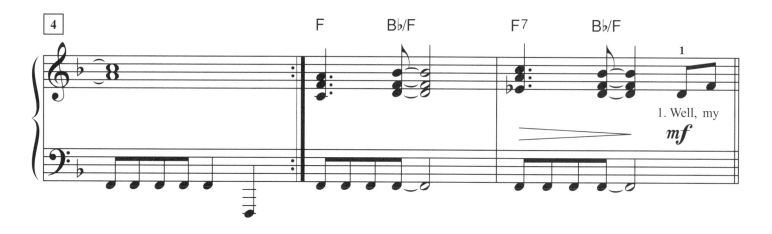

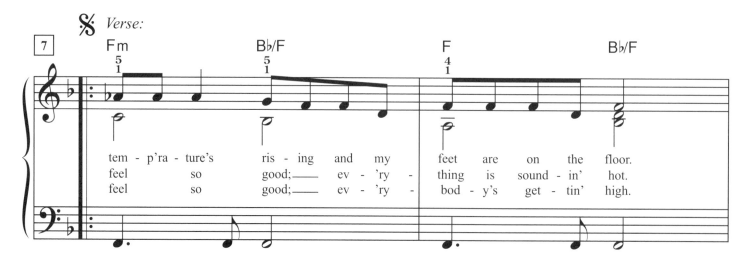

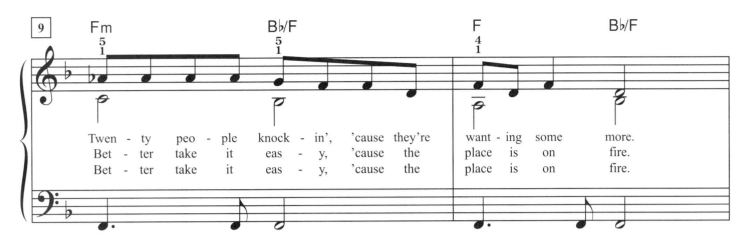

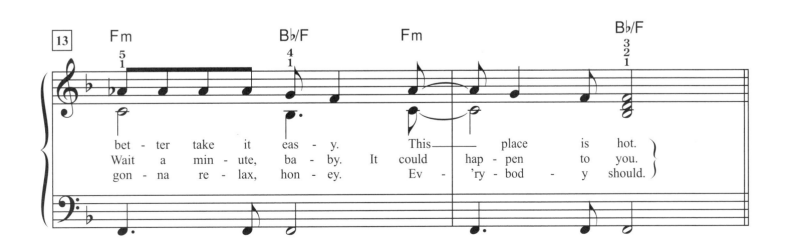

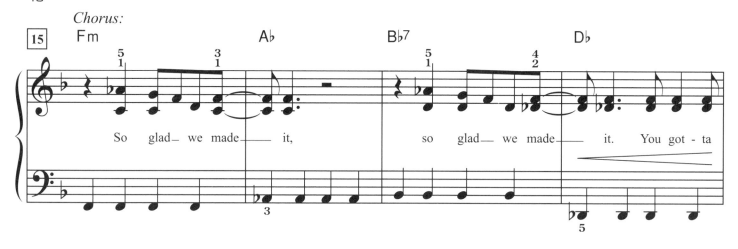

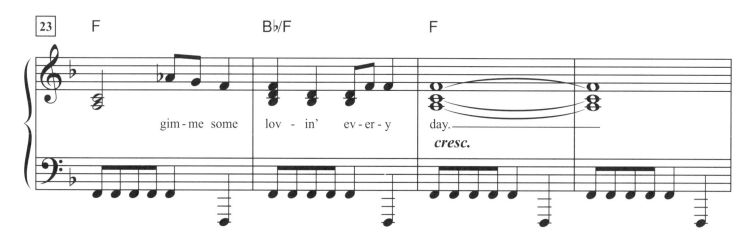

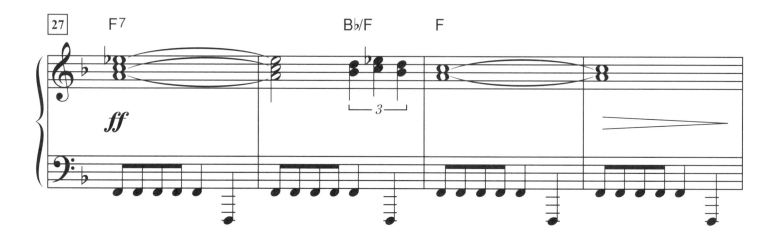

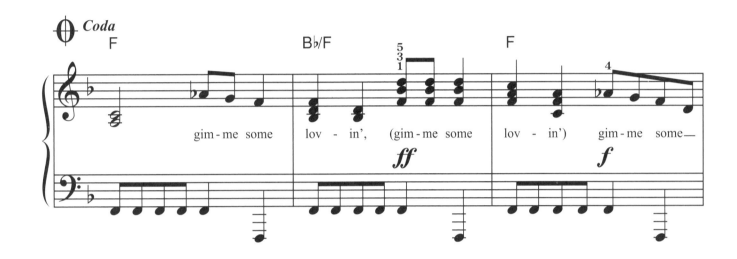

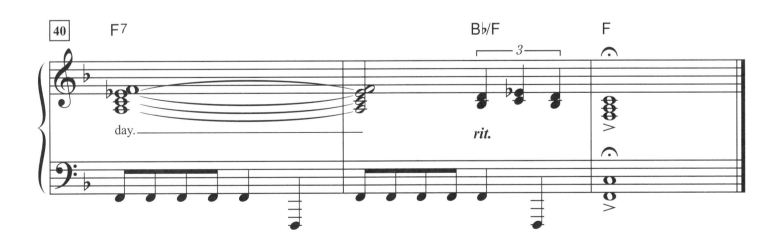

GOLDFINGER
(MAIN TITLE)

Goldfinger, the third movie in the long chain of James Bond films, was released in 1964. The title villain, played by Gert Fröbe, is a wealthy and crazed man obsessed with carrying out "Operation Grand Slam," a ploy to irradiate the U.S. gold supply. Bond, James Bond to be exact, foils Goldfinger's scheme in the end, being the only one of the two to successfully survive an infamous jet ride.

Music by John Barry
Lyrics by Leslie Bricusse and Anthony Newley
Arranged by Dan Coates

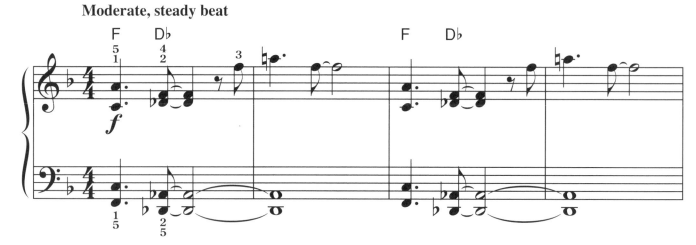

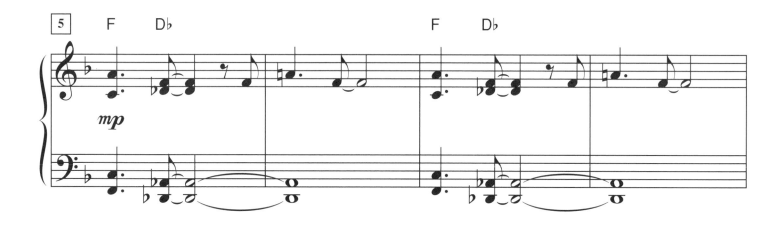

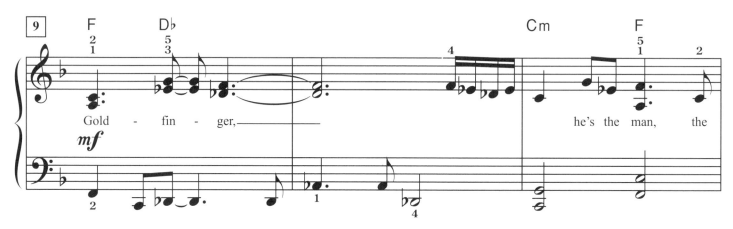

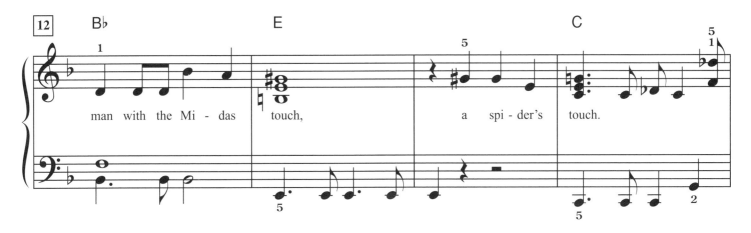

man with the Mi - das touch, a spi - der's touch.

Such a cold fin - ger

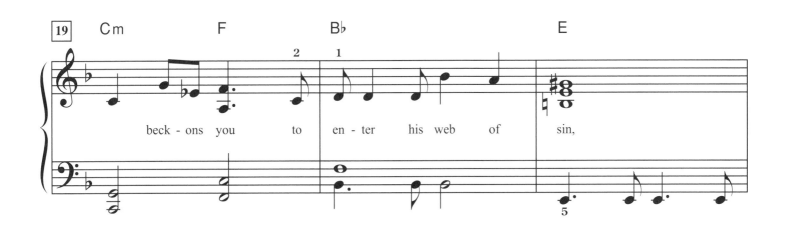

beck - ons you to en - ter his web of sin,

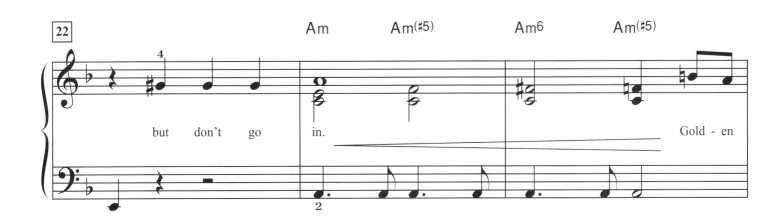

but don't go in. Gold - en

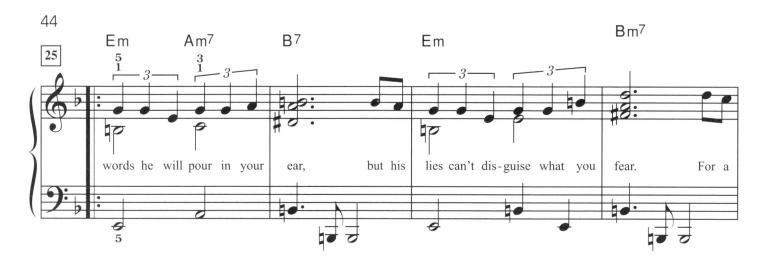

words he will pour in your ear, but his lies can't dis-guise what you fear. For a

gold - en girl knows when he's kissed her. It's the kiss of death from Mis - ter

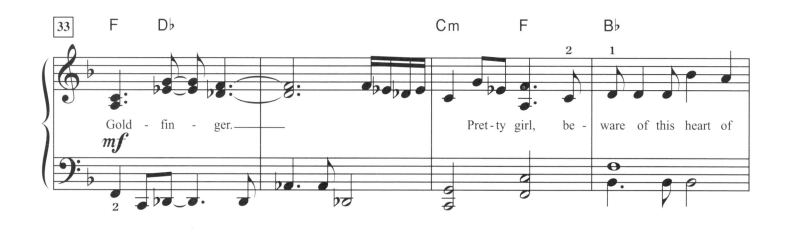

Gold - fin - ger. _____ Pret-ty girl, be - ware of this heart of

_mf_

gold. This heart is cold. _cresc._ Gold - en

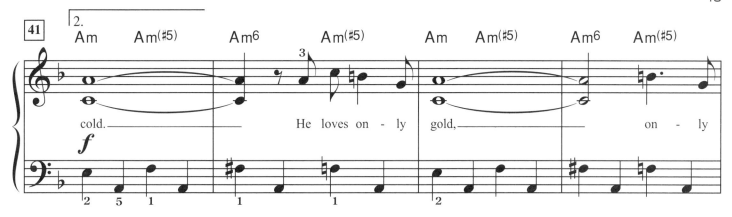

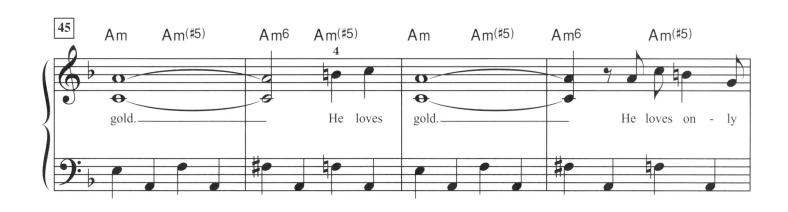

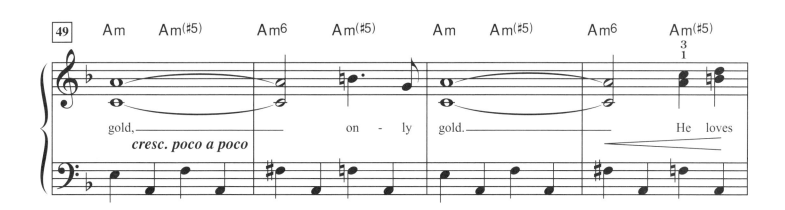

(YOUR LOVE HAS LIFTED ME) HIGHER AND HIGHER

"(Your Love Has Lifted Me) Higher and Higher" was recorded originally by Jackie Wilson in 1967. It was on the Billboard Top 40 singles chart for 12 weeks, peaking at #6 and has been used in a variety of movies: *Ghostbusters II*, *The Air Up There*, and *Death to Smoochy*.

Words and Music by
Gary Jackson, Carl Smith and Raynard Miner
Arranged by Dan Coates

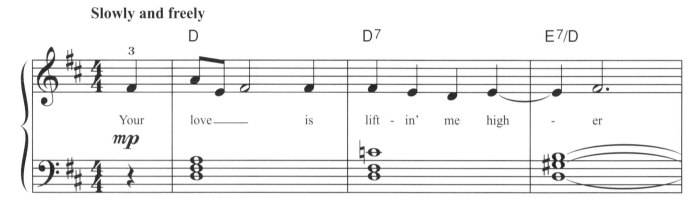

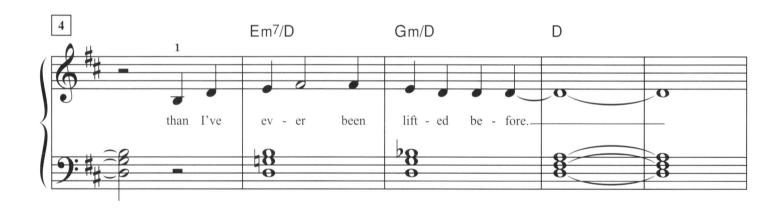

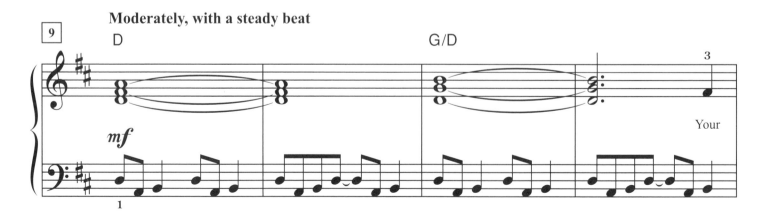

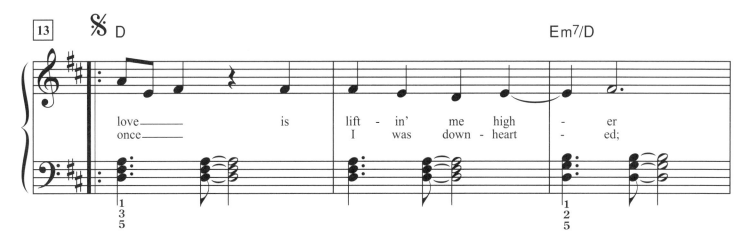

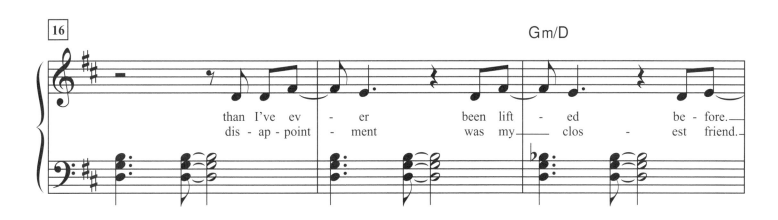

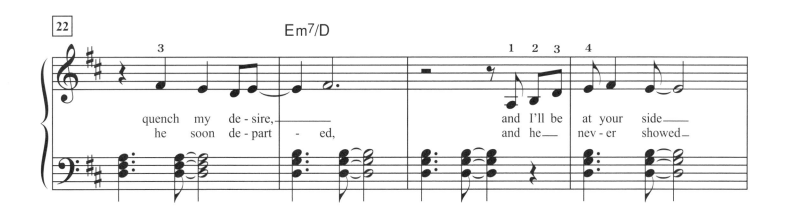

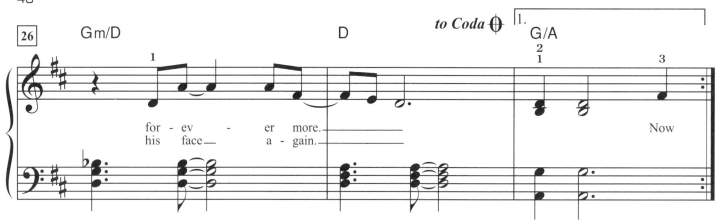

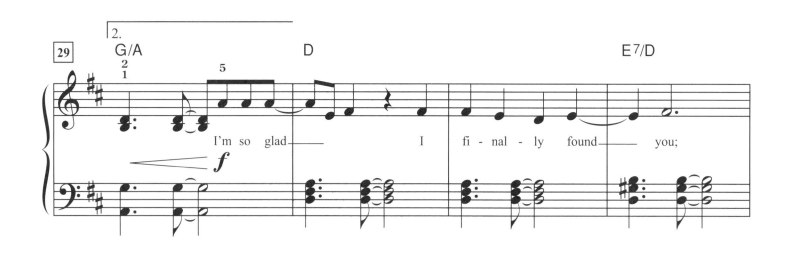

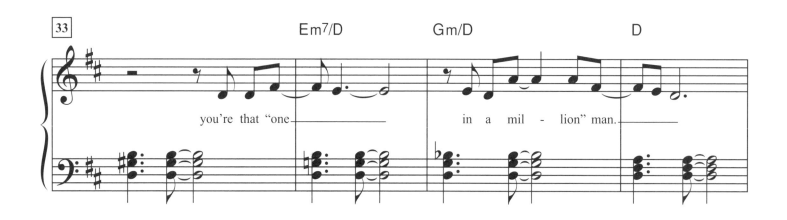

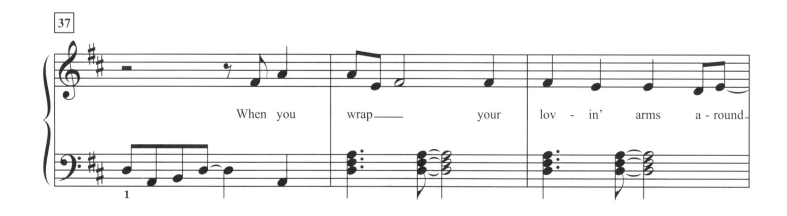

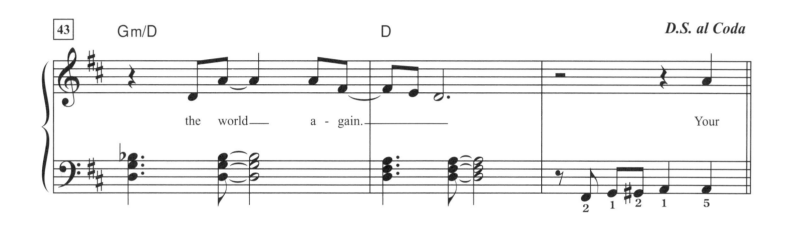

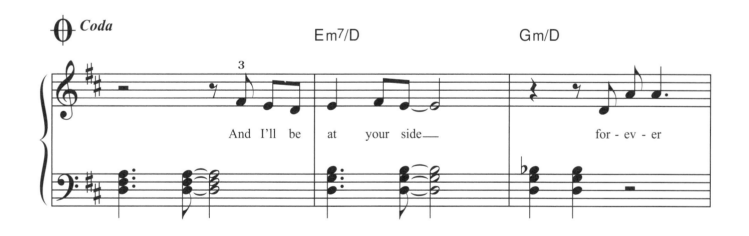

I ONLY WANT TO BE WITH YOU

Before the Beatles arrived in America, British singer Dusty Springfield came out with "I Only Want to Be with You." She released it in November of 1963, and it reached the top of the charts in Great Britain and the U.S. It has been used in a number of settings, including the *Ally McBeal* soundtrack.

Words and Music by
Mike Hawker and Ivor Raymonde
Arranged by Dan Coates

Bright dance tempo

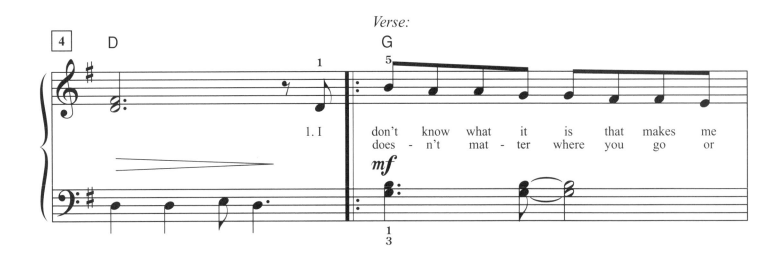

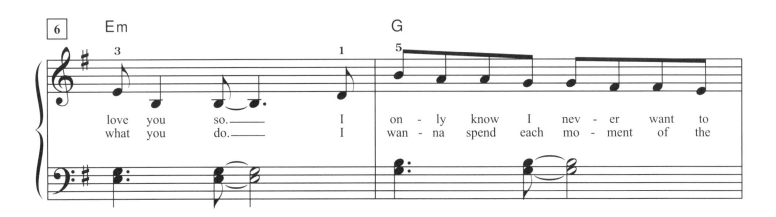

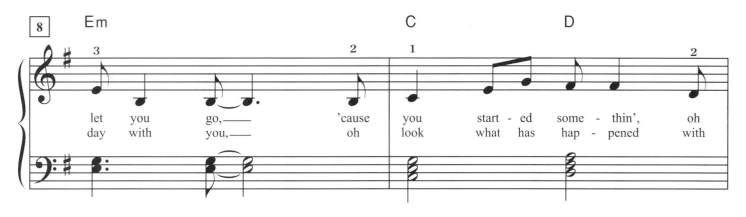

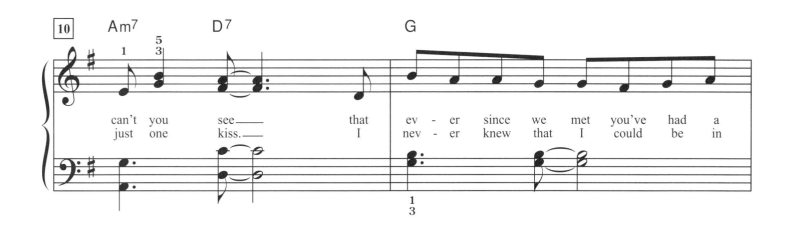

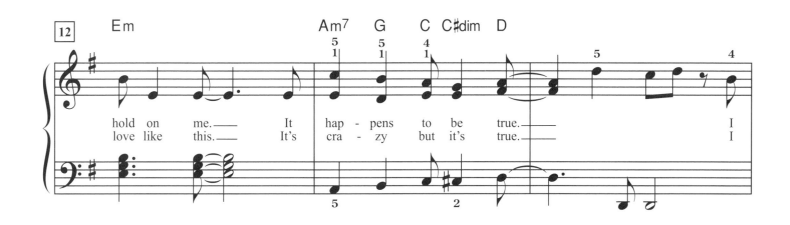

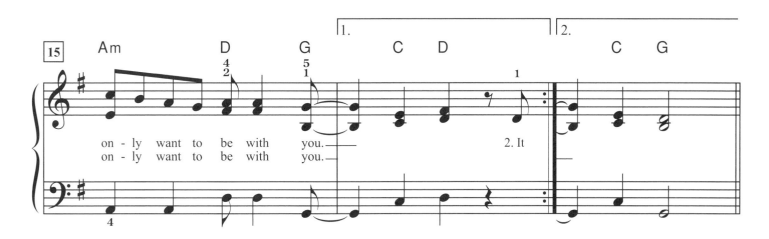

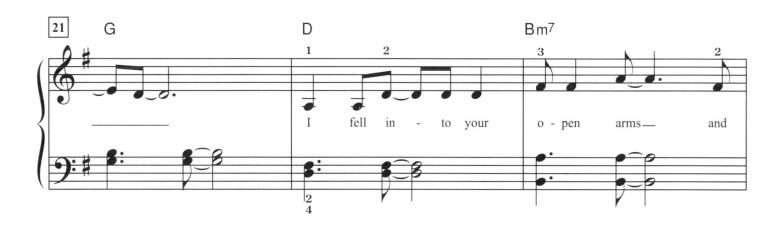

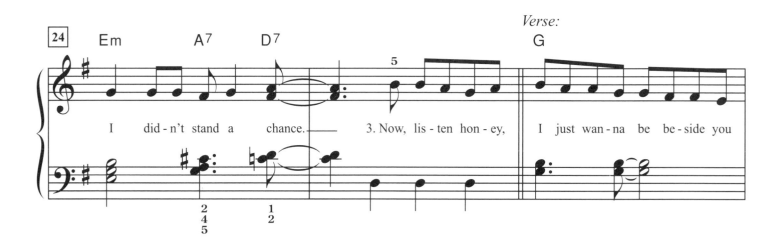

53

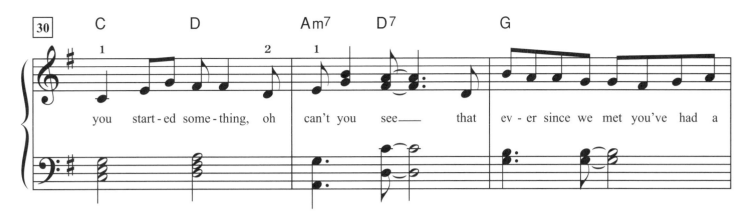

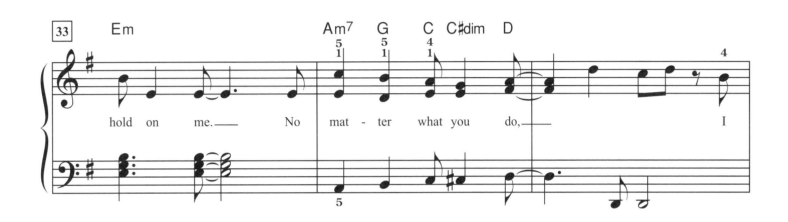

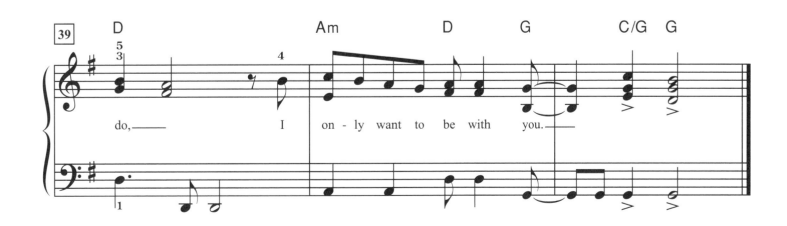

IF I RULED THE WORLD

"If I Ruled the World" originated in the 1963 musical, *Pickwick*, based on Charles Dickens's first novel, *The Pickwick Papers* (a.k.a. *The Posthumous Papers of the Pickwick Club*). The story centers on Mr. Samuel Pickwick, who travels throughout the English countryside with a group of companions. "If I Ruled the World" is a song Pickwick sings when he is mistaken for an election candidate. A number of singers have covered the song including Tony Bennett and Celine Dion, James Brown and Stevie Wonder.

Music by Cyril Ornadel
Words by Leslie Bricusse
Arranged by Dan Coates

Slowly, with expression

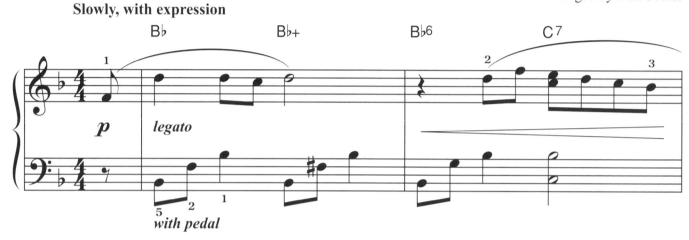

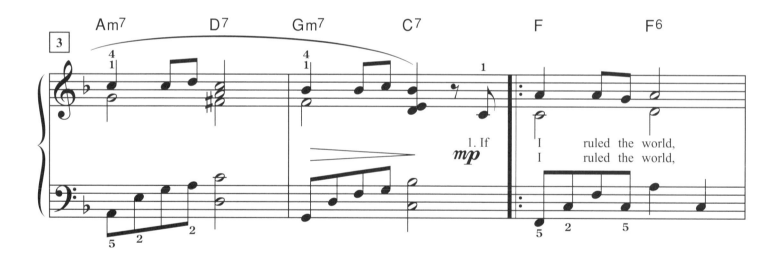

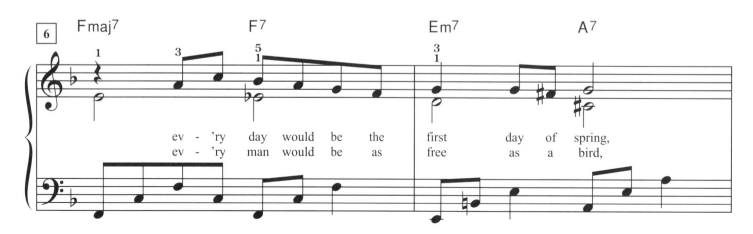

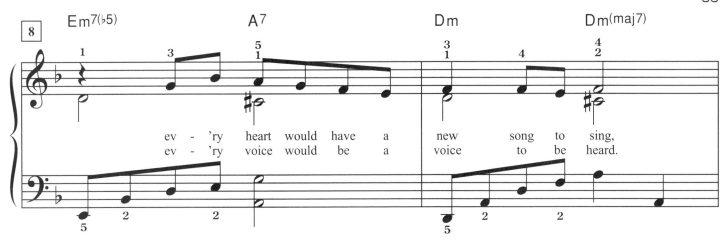

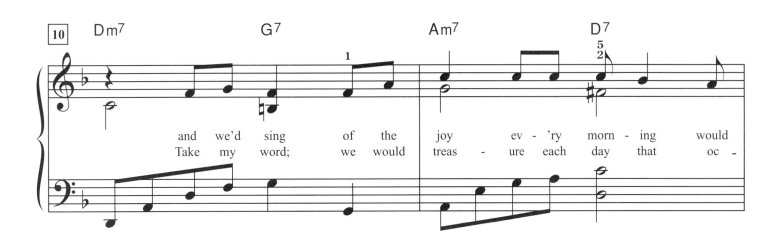

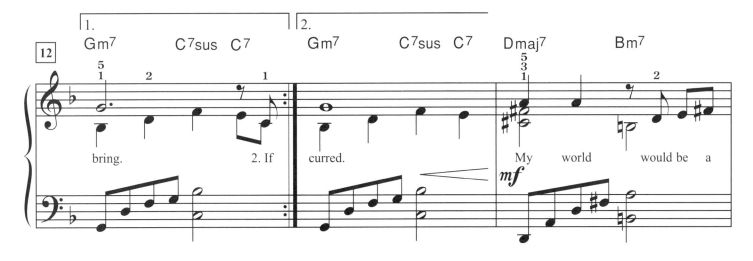

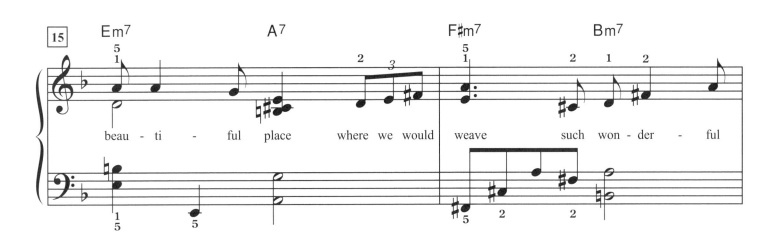

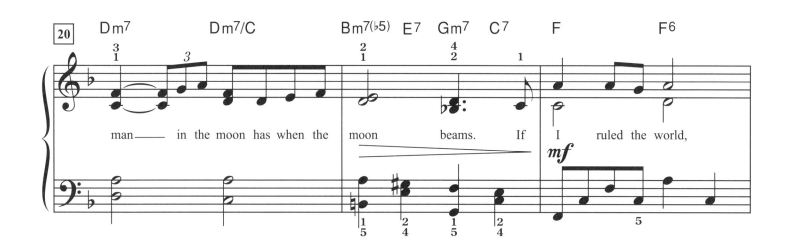

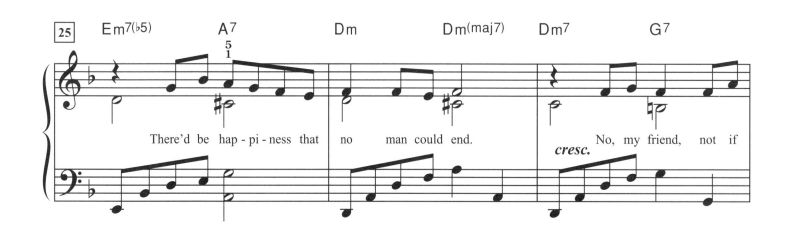

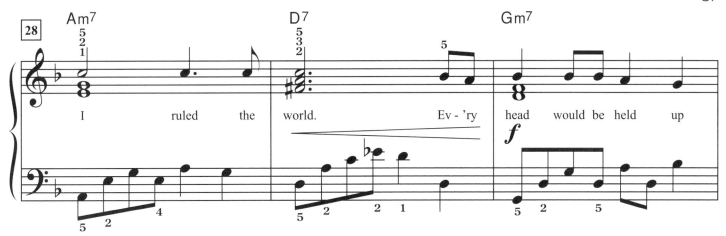

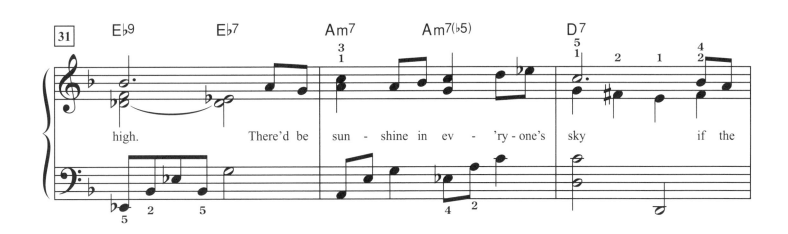

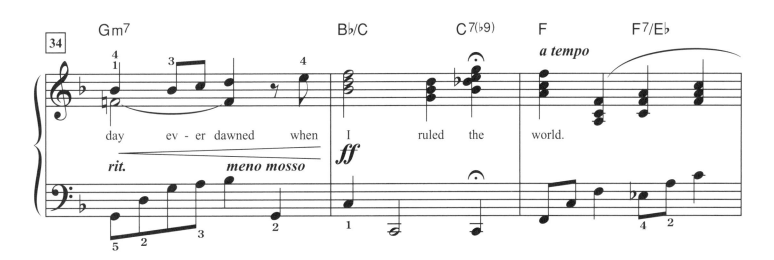

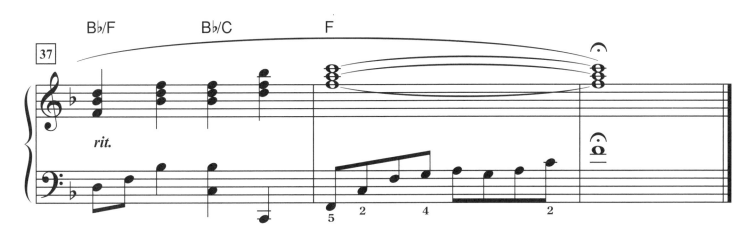

IT WAS A VERY GOOD YEAR

"It Was a Very Good Year" is a song about a man who remembers his relationships over the years, ultimately concluding they've all been sweet and fine (as vintage wine, hence the title). Frank Sinatra won a Grammy for his 1966 recording, and it has been covered by everyone from William Shatner, to Robbie Williams, to Homer Simpson ("It Was a Very Good Beer").

Words and Music by Ervin Drake
Arranged by Dan Coates

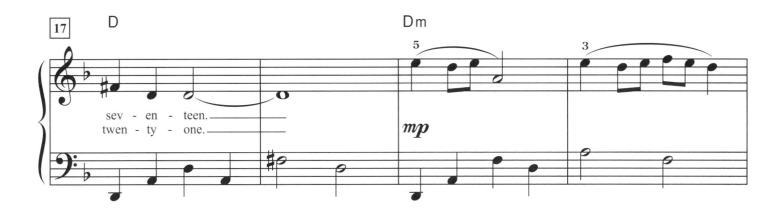

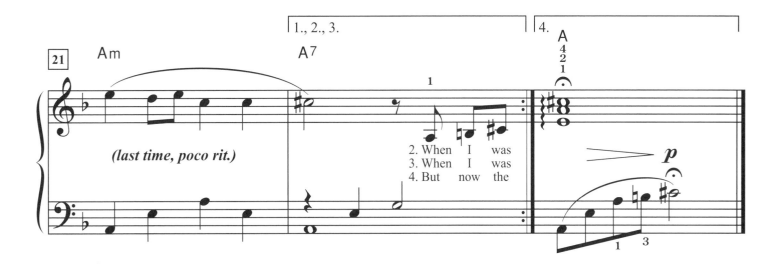

Verse 3:
When I was thirty-five, it was a very good year,
It was a very good year for blue-blooded girls of independent means.
We'd ride in limousines their chauffeurs would drive
When I was thirty-five.

Verse 4:
But now the days are short, I'm in the autumn of the year,
And now I think of my life as vintage wine from the old kegs.
From the brim to the dregs it poured sweet and clear;
It was a very good year.

IT'S MY PARTY

Lesley Gore popularized "It's My Party" in 1963. Although it was Gore's only hit in the U.S., it reached #1 on both the pop and R & B charts. Gore also recorded a sequel to "It's My Party" entitled "Judy's Turn to Cry" in which the narrator of the first song gets revenge.

Words and Music by
Herb Wiener, John Gluck and Wally Gold
Arranged by Dan Coates

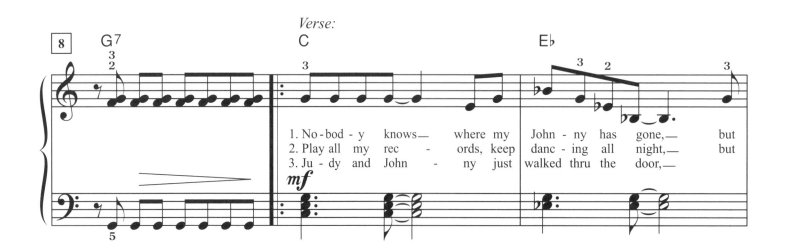

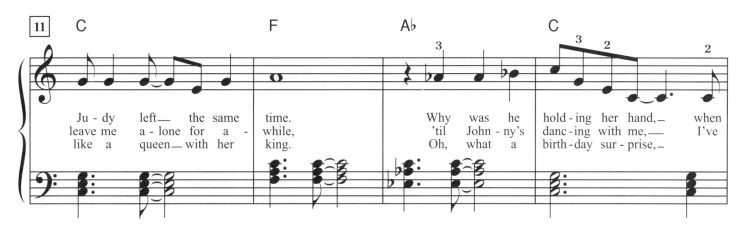

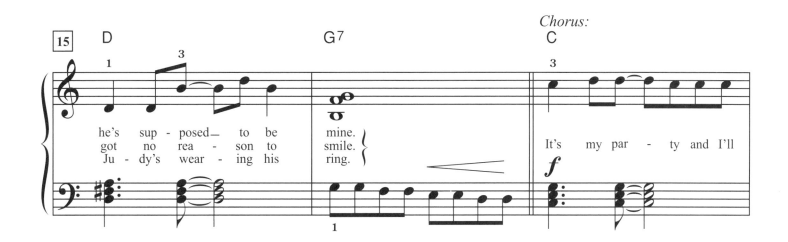

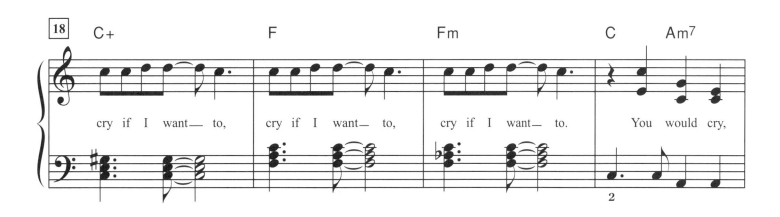

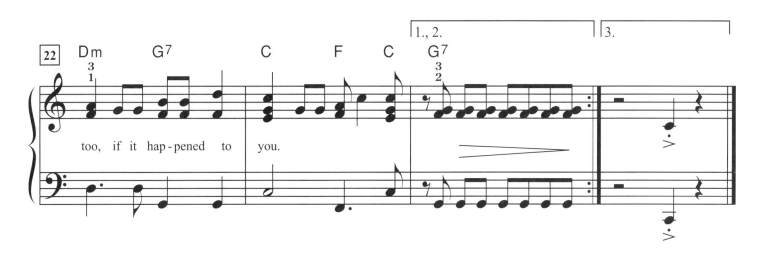

ITSY BITSY TEENIE WEENIE YELLOW POLKA DOT BIKINI

Novelty songs are intentionally humorous and are often huge hits. "Itsy Bitsy Teenie Weenie Yellow Polka Dot Bikini" is a quintessential novelty song, having hit #1 on the Billboard Hot 100 in 1960 and making the top 10 in other countries. It is tremendously catchy and addresses a universal theme not commonly addressed in most pop songs—embarrassment.

Words and Music by
Paul J. Vance and Lee Pockriss
Arranged by Dan Coates

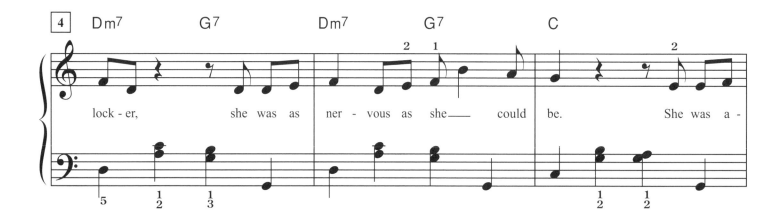

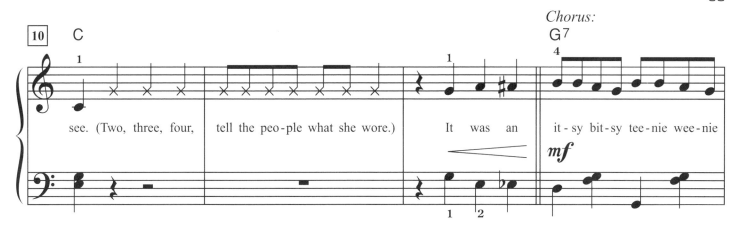

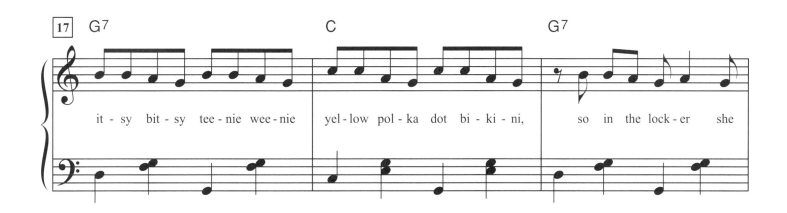

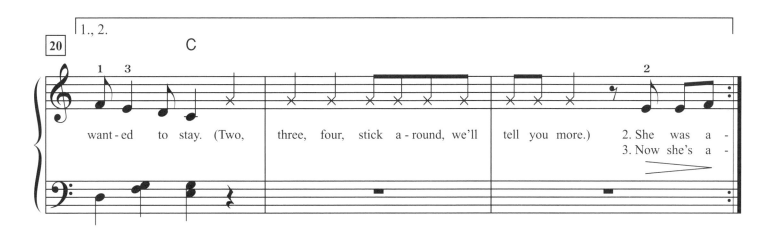

64

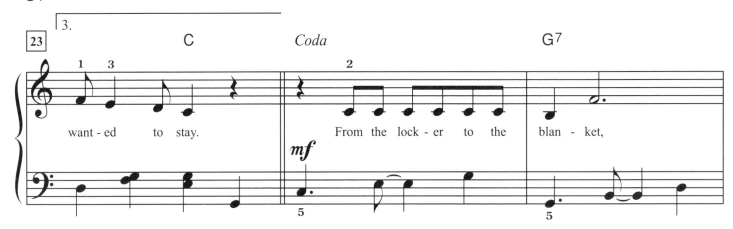

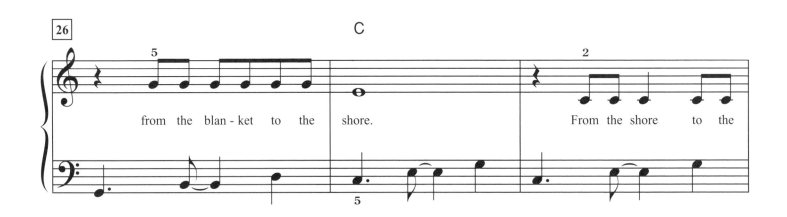

Verse 2:
She was afraid to come out in the open,
And so a blanket around her she wore.
She was afraid to come out in the open,
And so she sat bundled up on the shore.
(Two, three, four, tell the people what she wore.)
(To Chorus:)

Verse 3:
Now she's afraid to come out of the water,
And I wonder what she's gonna do.
Now she's afraid to come out of the water,
And the poor little girl's turning blue.
(Two, three, four, tell the people what she wore.)
(To Chorus:)

JAMES BOND THEME

The "James Bond Theme" first appeared in 1962 in *Dr. No*, the first of the James Bond films. Since then the instrumentation has varied from electric guitar to symphony orchestra to Moog synthesizer and has had influences from disco to electronica. It evolved throughout the series and has reflected the lead character and the era of each movie.

By Monty Norman
Arranged by Dan Coates

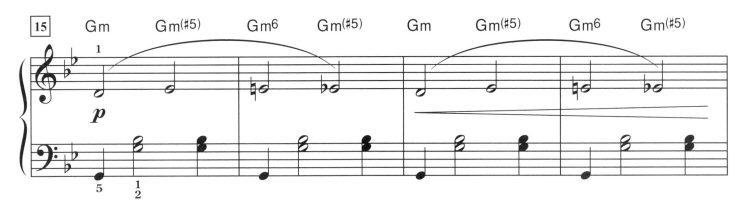

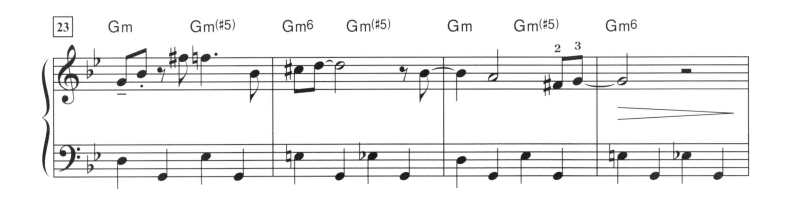

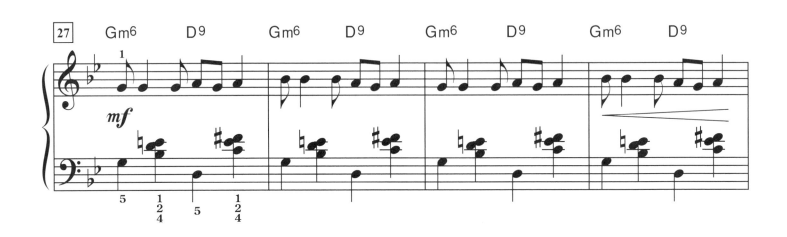

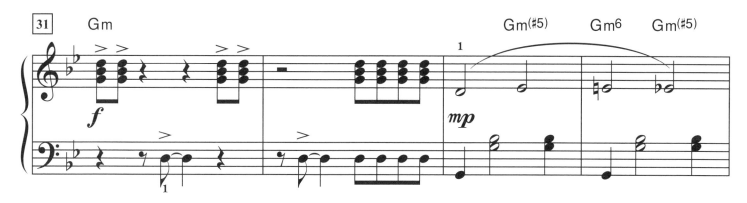

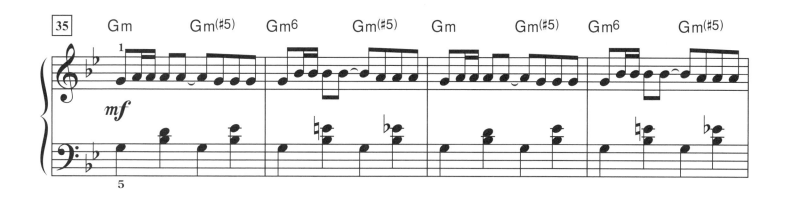

JOHNNY ANGEL

Shelley Fabares, known for her roles as Donna Reed's eldest daughter on *The Donna Reed Show* and as Coach's wife on the sitcom *Coach*, recorded "Johnny Angel" in 1962. It stayed 15 weeks on the charts peaking at #1. Her backup singers were Darlene Love and the Blossoms. Lee Pockriss, who wrote the music, is also the composer of "Itsy Bitsy Teenie Weenie Yellow Polka Dot Bikini" (on page 62).

Words by Lyn Duddy
Music by Lee Pockriss
Arranged by Dan Coates

LEAVING ON A JET PLANE

Peter, Paul and Mary's huge 1969 hit single, "Leaving on a Jet Plane," was written by John Denver in an airport in Washington in 1967 while on a layover. Its original title was "Oh Babe I Hate to Go" but was changed by Denver at the suggestion of his producer, Milt Okun.

Words and Music by John Denver
Arranged by Dan Coates

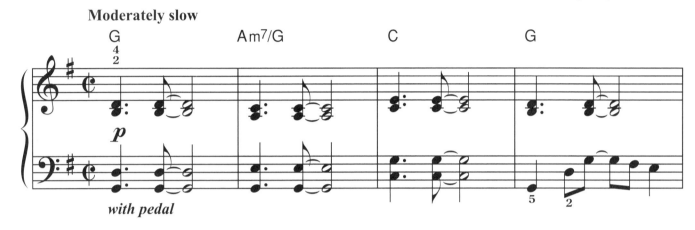

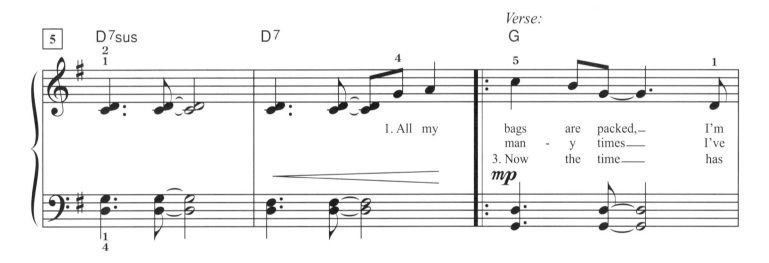

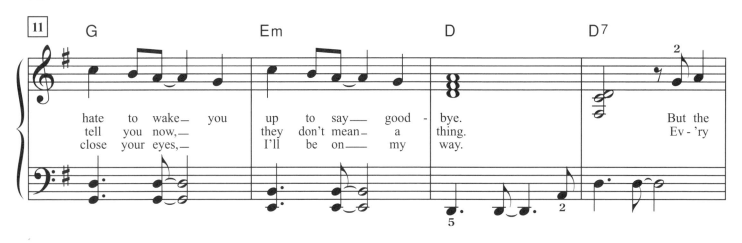

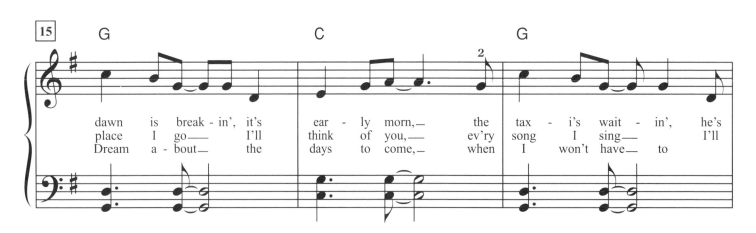

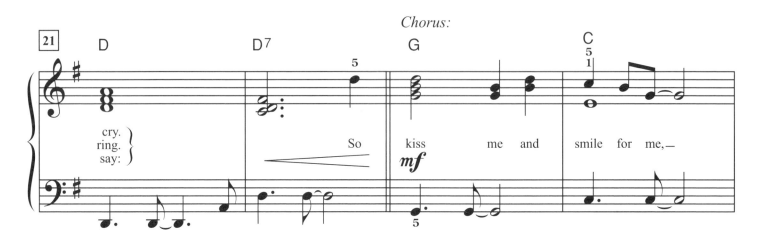

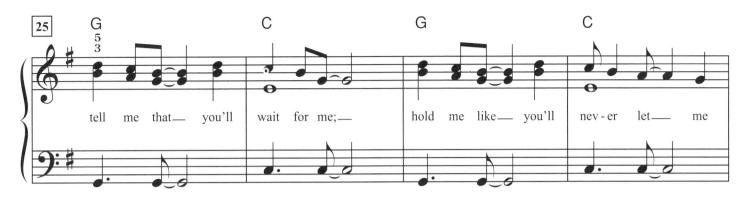

tell me that__ you'll wait for me;__ hold me like__ you'll nev-er let__ me

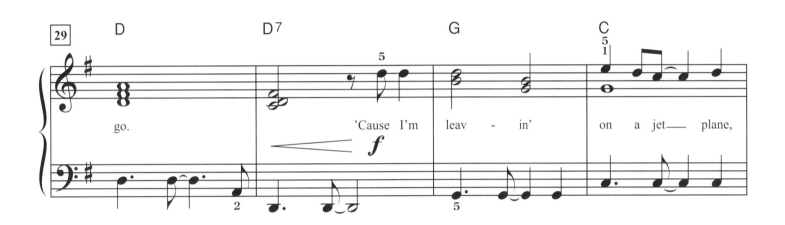

go. 'Cause I'm leav - in' on a jet__ plane,

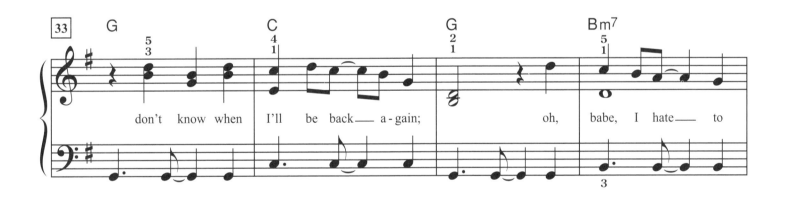

don't know when I'll be back__ a-gain; oh, babe, I hate__ to

go. 2. There's so go. rit. e dim.

THE LION SLEEPS TONIGHT

Despite a rocky copyright history—a *Rolling Stone* exposé, a PBS documentary, a $1.6 million dollar lawsuit—"The Lion Sleeps Tonight" (originally titled "Mbube" and later recorded as "Wimoweh") has been an international success. There have been many recorded versions of the song. The Tokens, a doo-wop group from Brooklyn, made a recording of it in 1961 that topped the charts at #1.

New Lyric and Revised Music by
George David Weiss, Hugo Peretti and Luigi Creatore
Arranged by Dan Coates

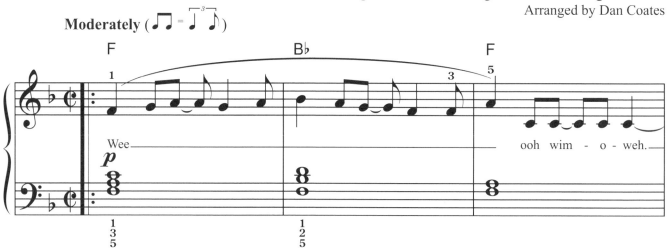

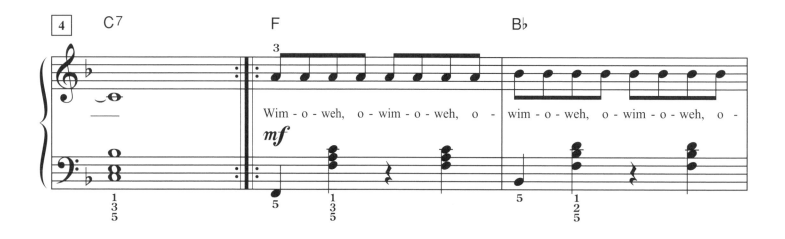

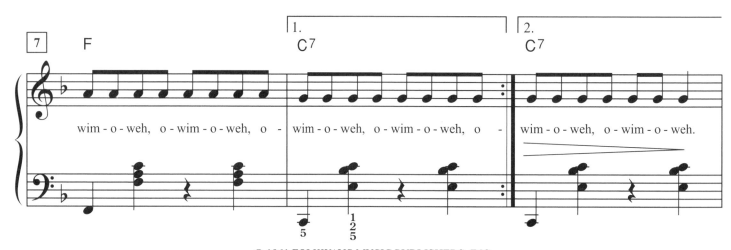

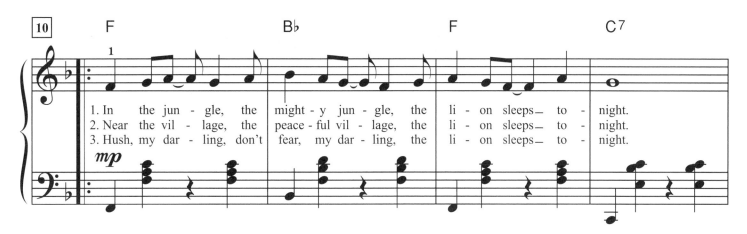

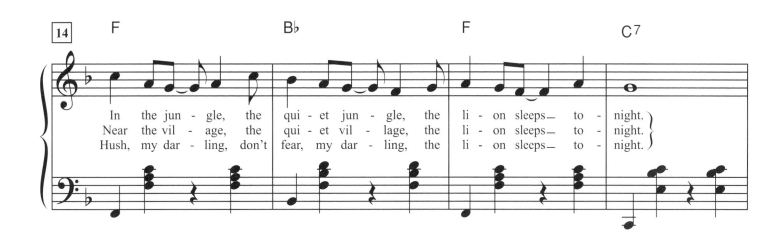

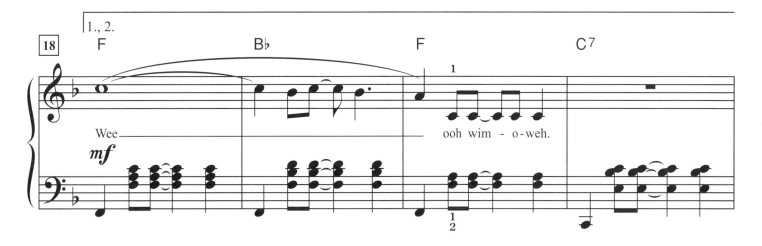

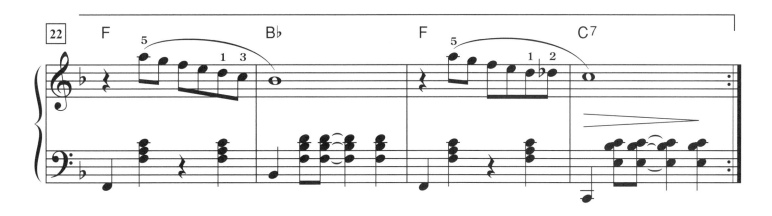

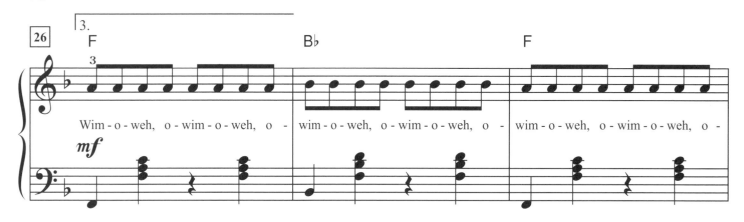

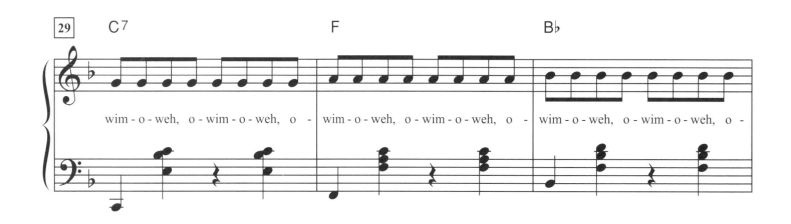

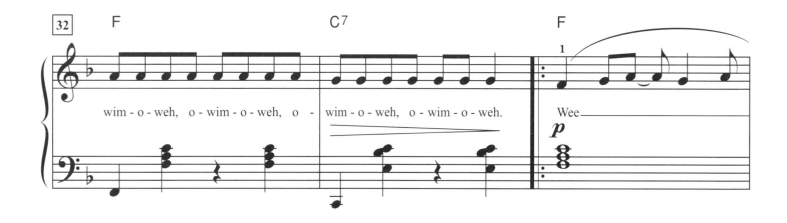

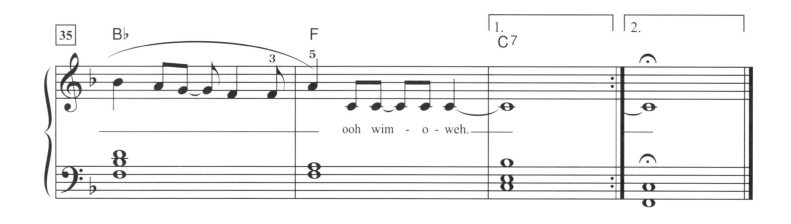

MAKE SOMEONE HAPPY

"Make Someone Happy" originated in the musical *Do Re Mi*, a story about a con man who decides to go into the music business. The show opened on Broadway in 1960, and the song was introduced to the public as a second act duet. Jimmy Durante—one of America's most-loved entertainers, known for his gravely voice and large nose—recorded it as a solo, which can be heard during the closing credits of the famous romantic comedy *Sleepless in Seattle*.

Lyrics by Betty Comden and Adolph Green
Music by Jule Styne
Arranged by Dan Coates

Moderately, with a steady beat

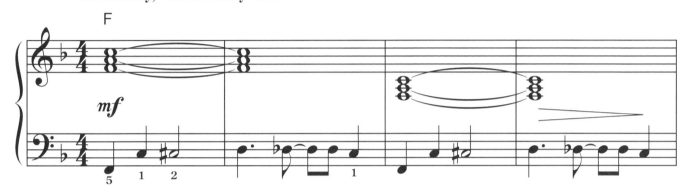

Make_____ some-one hap - py, make just one___ some-one hap - py.

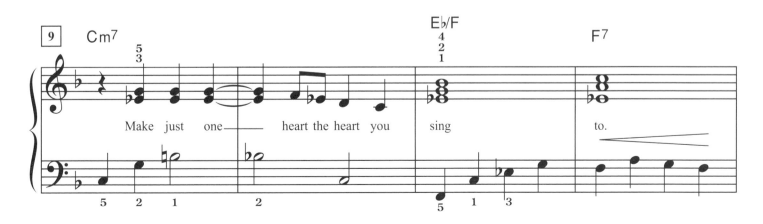

Make just one___ heart the heart you sing to.

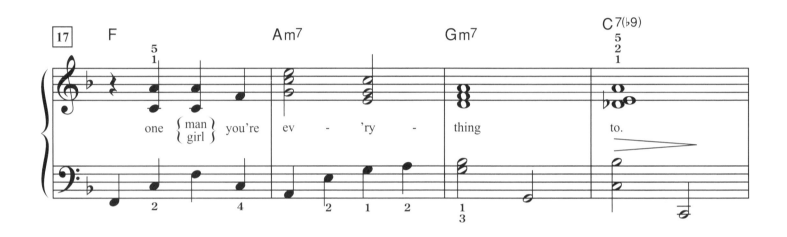

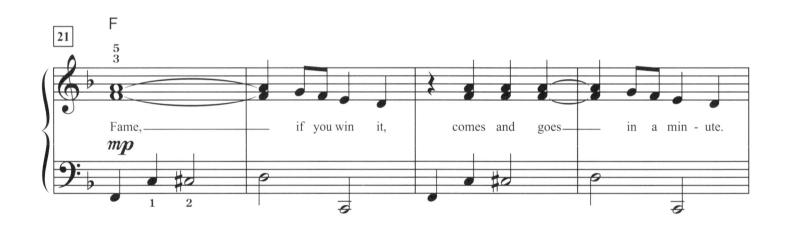

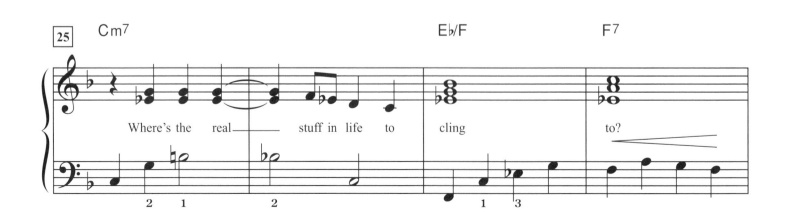

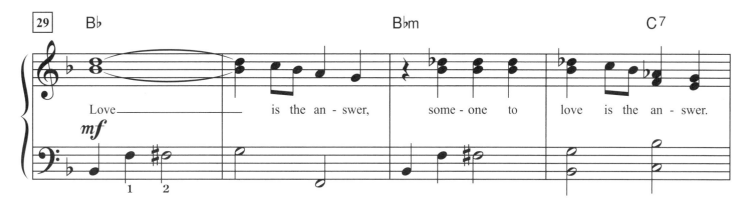

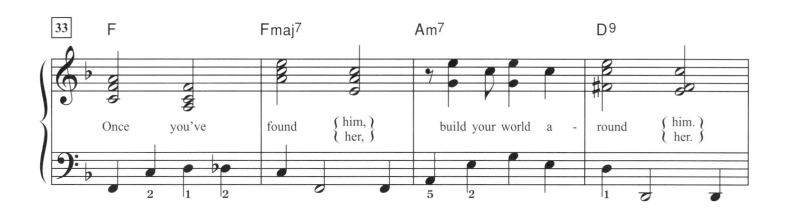

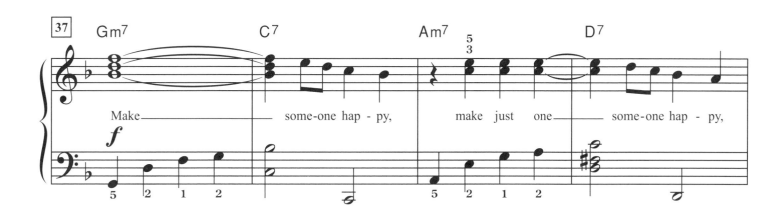

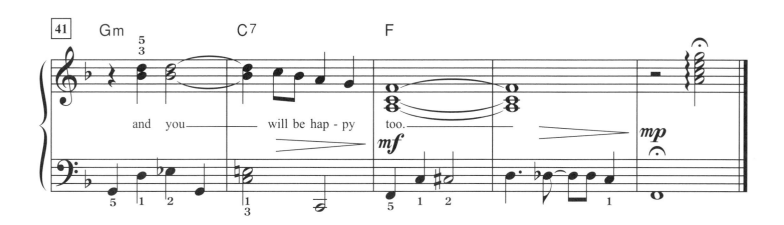

MR. BOJANGLES

The character Mr. Bojangles has found his way into such diverse works as Philip Glass's opera *Einstein on the Beach* and *The Simpsons* episode "Milhouse Doesn't Live Here Anymore." As the story goes, Bojangles is a vagabond folk dancer who would travel throughout the southern United States. Jerry Jeff Walker wrote this song about a mysterious and talented prison inmate in 1968.

Words and Music by Jerry Jeff Walker
Arranged by Dan Coates

82

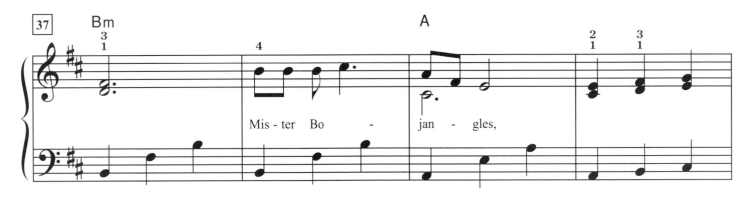

Mis - ter Bo - jan - gles,

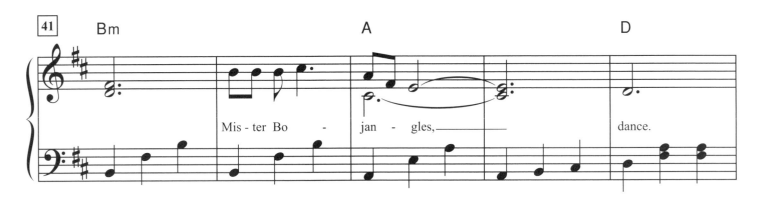

Mis - ter Bo - jan - gles,_____ dance.

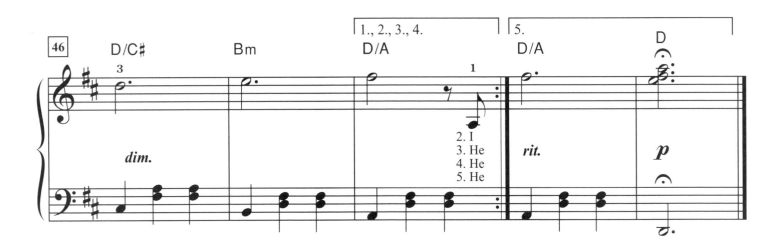

dim.

1., 2., 3., 4.

5.

rit.

p

2. I
3. He
4. He
5. He

Verse 2:
I met him in a cell in New Orleans
I was down and out.
He looked at me to be the eyes of age
As he spoke right out.
He talked of life, talked of life,
He laughed slapped his leg a step.
(To Chorus:)

Verse 3:
He said his name, Bojangles,
Then he danced a lick across the cell.
He grabbed his pants a better stance, oh, he jumped up high,
He clicked his heels.
He let go a laugh, let go a laugh,
Shook back his clothes all around.
(To Chorus:)

Verse 4:
He danced for those at minstrel shows and county fairs
Throughout the South.
He spoke with tears of fifteen years
How his dog and he traveled about.
His dog up and died, he up and died,
After twenty years he still grieved.
(To Chorus:)

Verse 5:
He said, "I dance now at every chance in honky tonks
For drinks and tips.
But most of the time I spend behind these county bars,"
He said, "I drinks a bit."
He shook his head, and as he shook his head,
I heard someone ask please...
(To Chorus:)

MRS. ROBINSON

Paul Simon and Art Garfunkel began working on "Mrs. Robinson" in 1967 while collaborating with director Mike Nichols on the film *The Graduate*. The song was not completed for the film but appears in the movie as incidental music. Simon and Garfunkel fleshed out the song and released it on their 1968 album *Bookends*. It quickly climbed to the top of the charts and became their second big hit after "The Sound of Silence."

Words and Music by Paul Simon
Arranged by Dan Coates

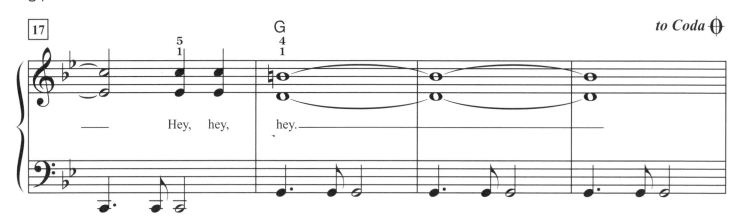

to Coda ⊕

Hey, hey, hey.

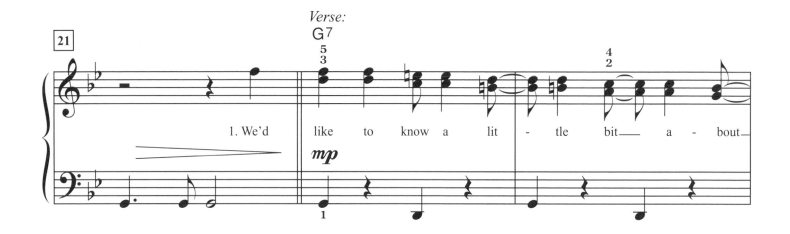

Verse:

1. We'd like to know a lit - tle bit a - bout

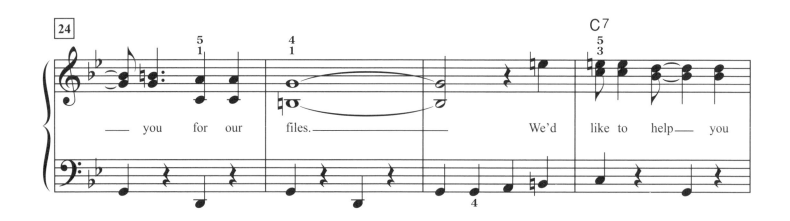

you for our files. We'd like to help you

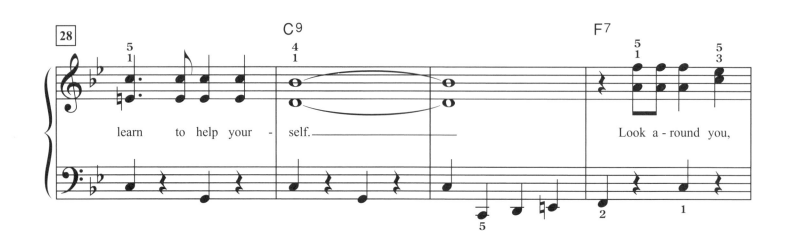

learn to help your - self. Look a - round you,

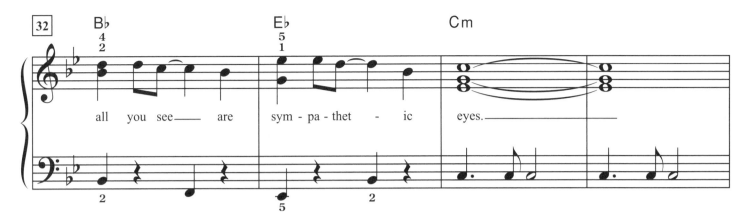

32 Bb / Eb / Cm

all you see___ are sym-pa-thet - ic eyes.___

36 G / F *D.S. al Coda*

Stroll a - round the grounds___ un - til you feel at home.___ And here's to

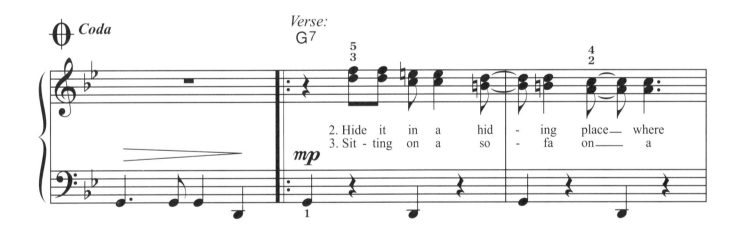

Coda / *Verse:* G7

2. Hide it in a hid - ing place___ where
3. Sit - ting on a so - fa on___ a

43 / C7

no one ev - er goes,___ put it in your pan -
Sun - day af - ter - noon,___ go - ing to the can -

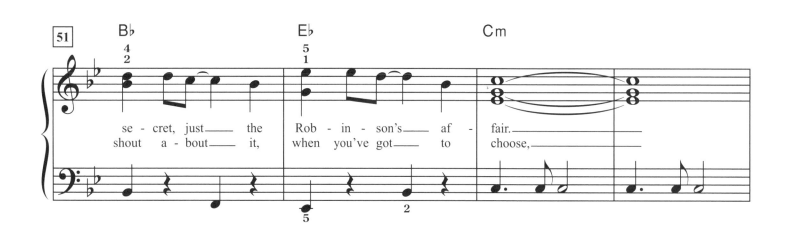

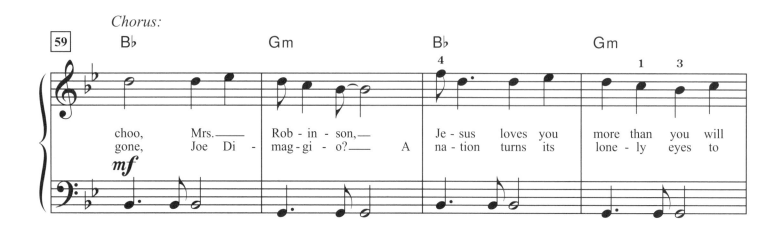

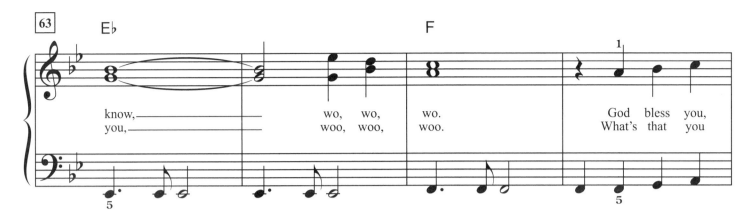

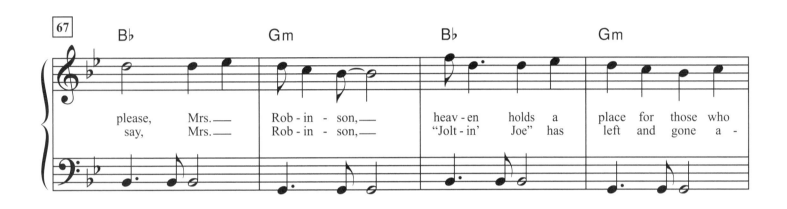

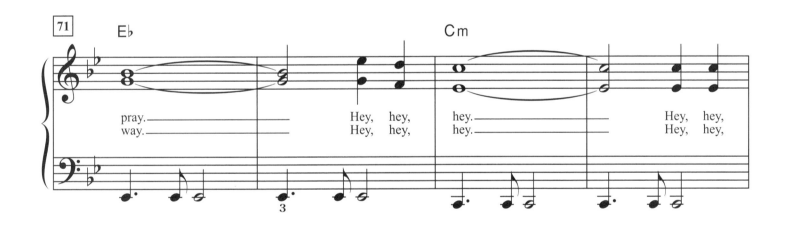

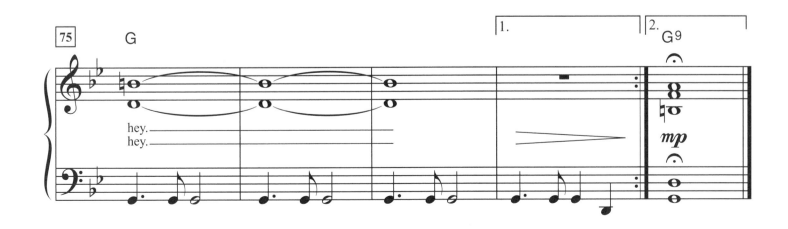

MY KIND OF TOWN
(CHICAGO IS)

"My Kind of Town (Chicago Is)" originated in *Robin and the 7 Hoods*, a 1964 musical film starring the members of the Rat Pack (Frank Sinatra, Dean Martin, Sammy Davis Jr.) as well as Bing Crosby, Peter Falk, Edward G. Robinson, and Barbara Rush. The song was nominated for an Academy Award and became a signature song for Sinatra.

Words by Sammy Cahn
Music by James Van Heusen
Arranged by Dan Coates

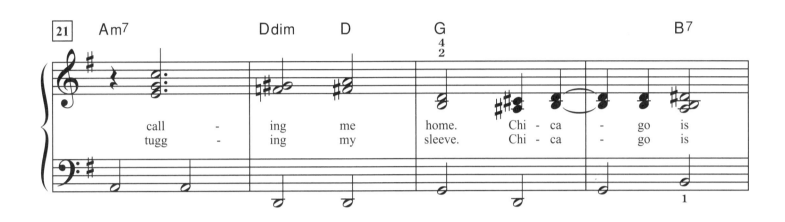

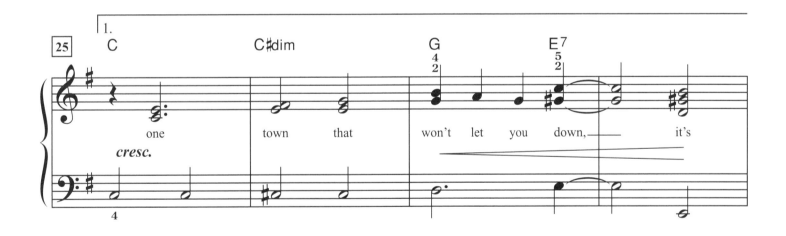

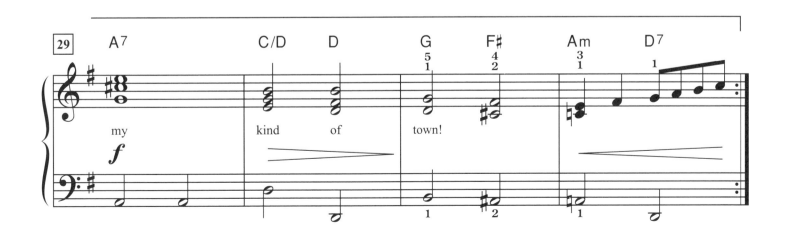

THE PINK PANTHER

The Pink Panther is a series of comedic films spanning the years 1963–2006. The main character is bumbling French detective, Jacques Clouseau (famously played by Peter Sellars in the earlier films), who manages to survive countless brushes with death despite his clumsiness and aloof demeanor. The jazzy theme is famous for its chromatically moving parallel fifths and furtive character.

Music by Henry Mancini
Arranged by Dan Coates

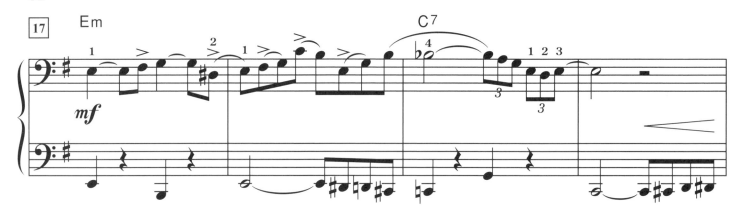

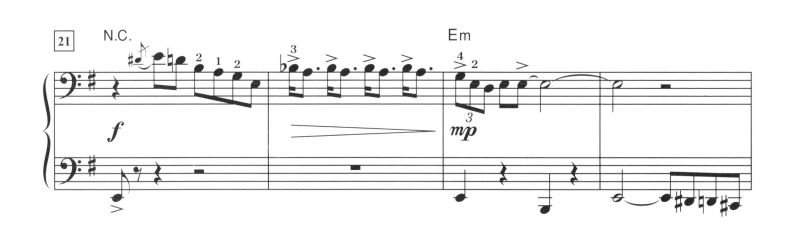

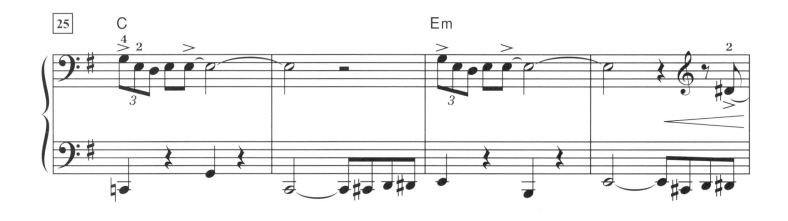

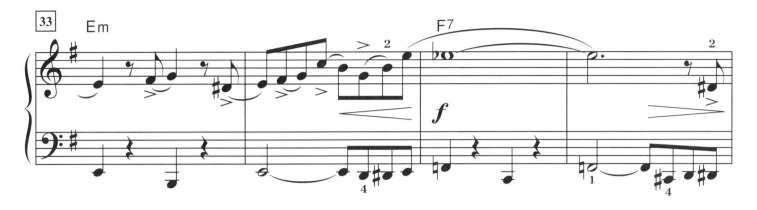

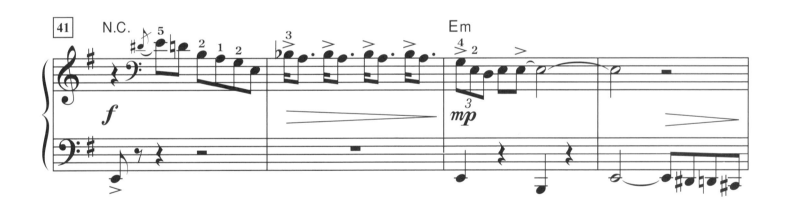

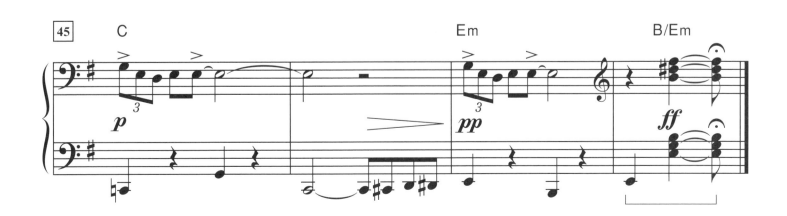

NEVER MY LOVE

"Sunshine pop" is a term used to describe light, optimistic rock music which mainly originated in California in the mid- to late-'60s. The Beach Boys, The Fifth Dimension, and The Mamas and the Papas are often associated with this style. The Association is another band of this genre, and they came out with their chart-topping "Never My Love" in 1967.

Words and Music by Don and Dick Addrisi
Arranged by Dan Coates

95

PEOPLE

Funny Girl opened on Broadway on March 26, 1964. It is the story of Fanny Brice, comedienne and singer, who tells her story in flashback: her beginnings in vaudeville, her romance with her husband Nick Arnstein, her stardom with the *Ziegfeld Follies*. Fanny sings "People" in Act I. Barbra Streisand played Fanny in the original cast and also in the 1968 screen adaptation. Although others have recorded it, "People" is considered one of Streisand's signature songs.

Words by Bob Merrill
Music by Jule Styne
Arranged by Dan Coates

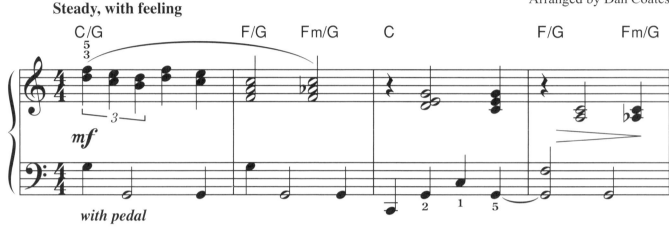

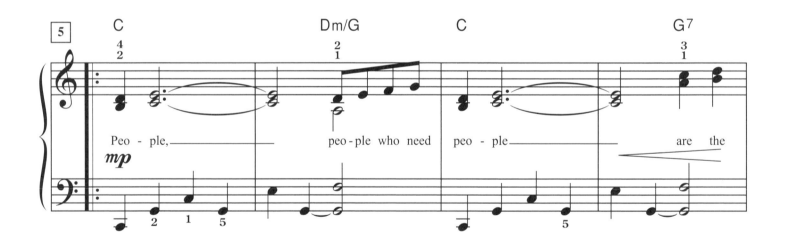

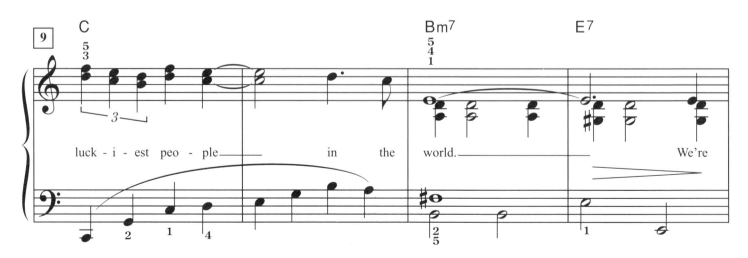

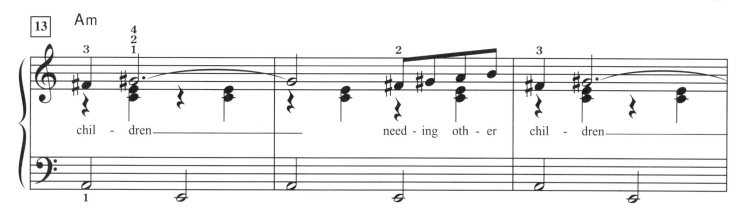

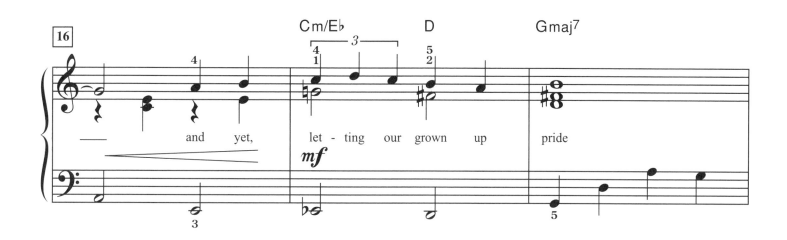

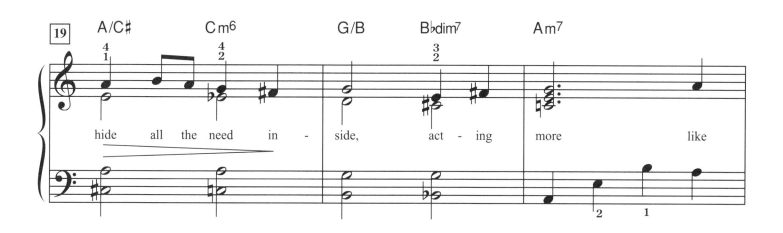

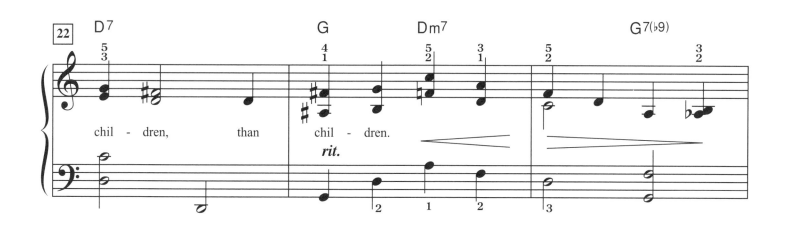

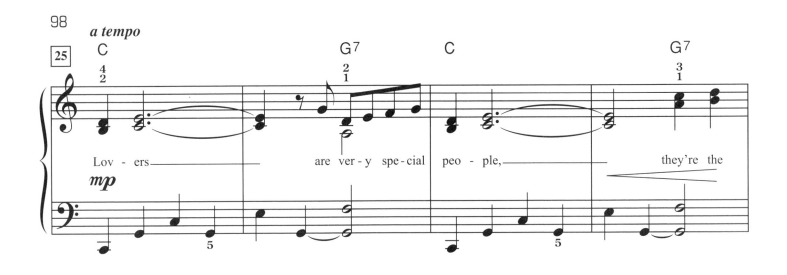

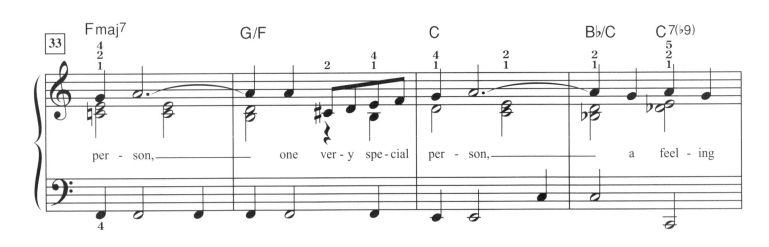

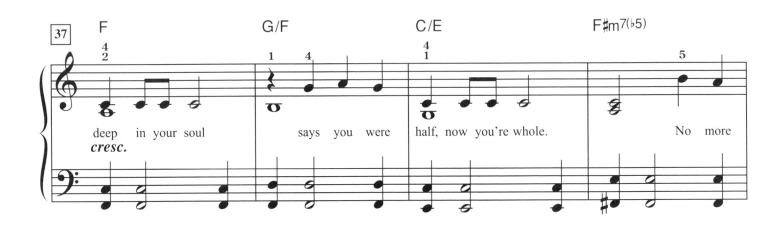

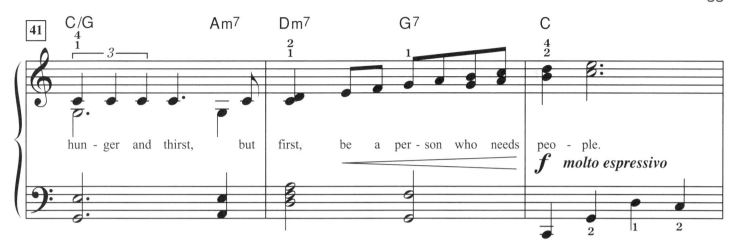

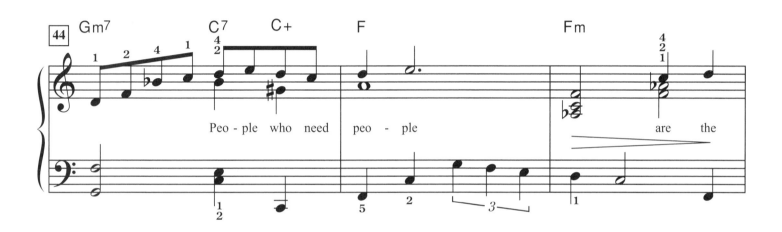

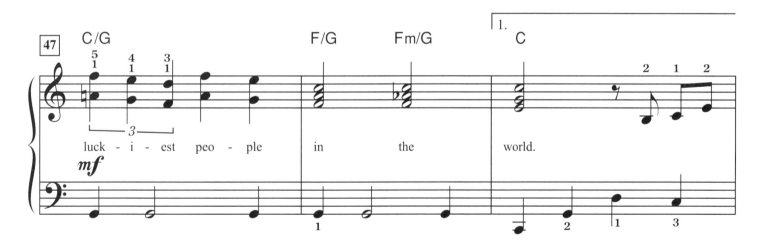

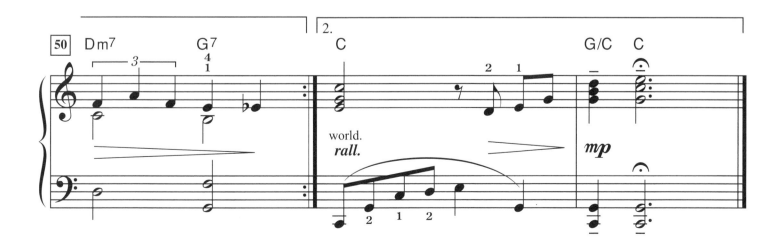

PUFF (THE MAGIC DRAGON)

"Puff (The Magic Dragon)" was written by two Cornell University friends, Leonard Lipton and Peter Yarrow. Peter would become the "Peter" of Peter, Paul and Mary, the group who made the song popular in 1963. Inspired by an Ogden Nash poem titled "Custard the Dragon," "Puff" tells the story of a magical dragon and his playmate, Jackie Paper. Despite a history of conflicting interpretations regarding its lyrics, the song has remained popular and even resulted in a series of animated television specials in the '70s aimed at helping troubled children.

Words and Music by
Peter Yarrow and Leonard Lipton
Arranged by Dan Coates

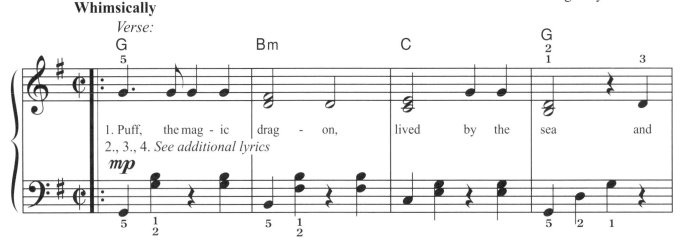

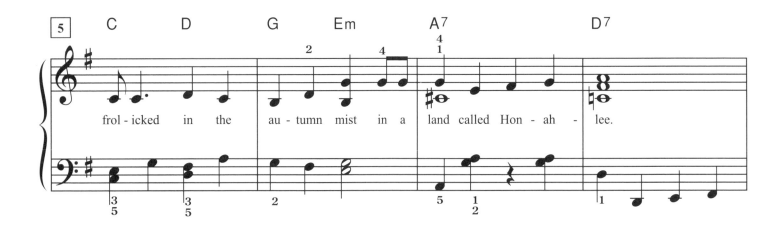

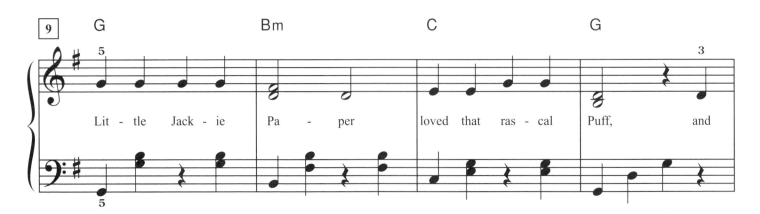

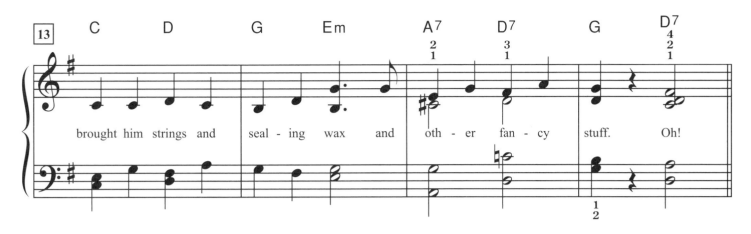

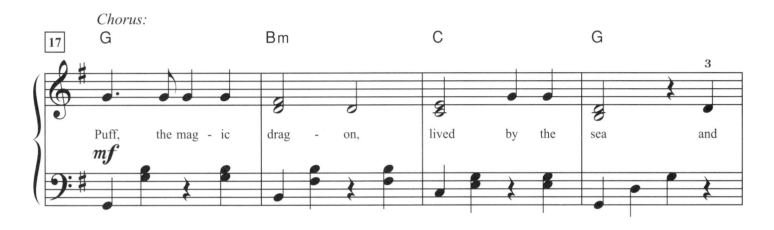

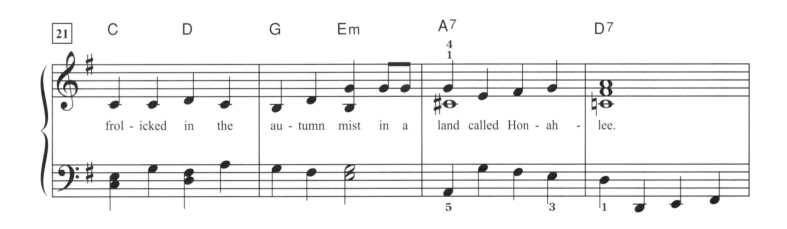

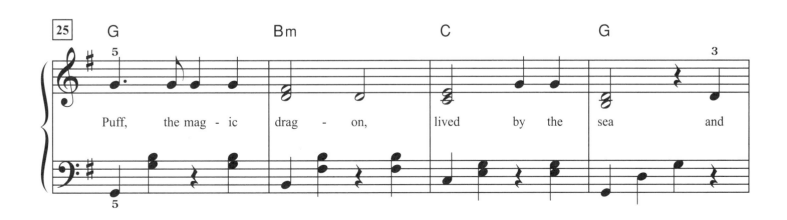

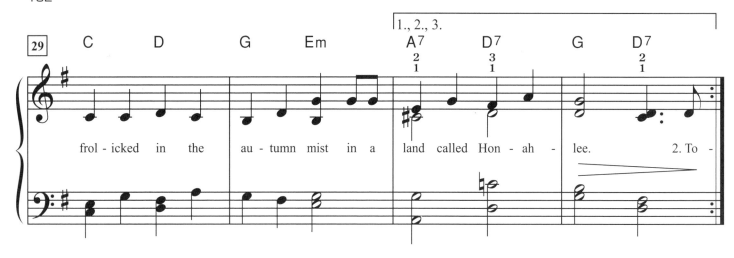

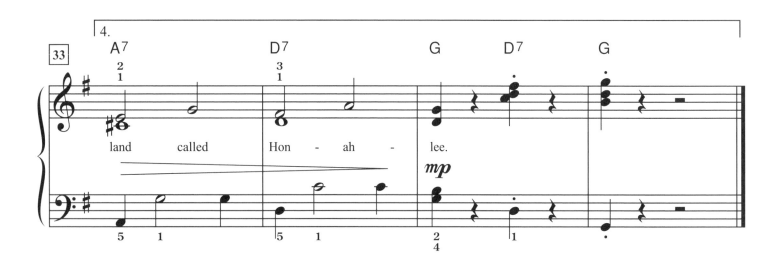

Verse 2:
Together they would travel on a boat with billowed sail,
Jackie left a lookout perched on Puff's gigantic tail.
Noble kings and princes would bow when e'er they came.
Pirate ships would low'r their flag when Puff roared out his name. Oh!
(To Chorus:)

Verse 3:
A dragon lives forever, but not so little boys;
Painted wings and giant rings make way for other toys.
One grey night it happened, Jackie Paper came no more.
And Puff, that mighty dragon, he ceased his fearless roar. Oh!
(To Chorus:)

Verse 4:
His head was bent in sorrow, green scales fell like rain,
Puff no longer went to play along the cherry lane.
Without his life-long friend, Puff could not be brave,
So Puff, that mighty dragon, sadly slipped into his cave. Oh!
(To Chorus:)

RAINDROPS KEEP FALLIN' ON MY HEAD

B. J. Thomas recorded "Raindrops Keep Fallin' on My Head" in 1969 for the movie *Butch Cassidy and the Sundance Kid*. It accompanies a dialogue-less scene in the film where Butch pursues Etta Place, Sundance's girlfriend. The song won the Academy Award in 1969 for Best Original Song and became a worldwide hit.

Words by Hal David
Music by Burt Bacharach
Arranged by Dan Coates

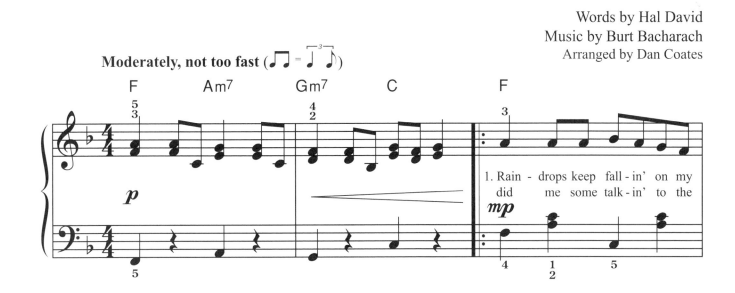

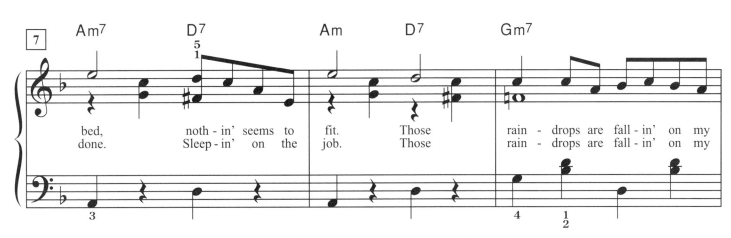

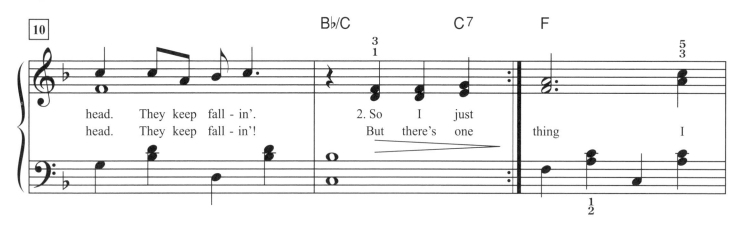

head. They keep fall - in'.
head. They keep fall - in'!

2. So   I   just
But there's one   thing   I

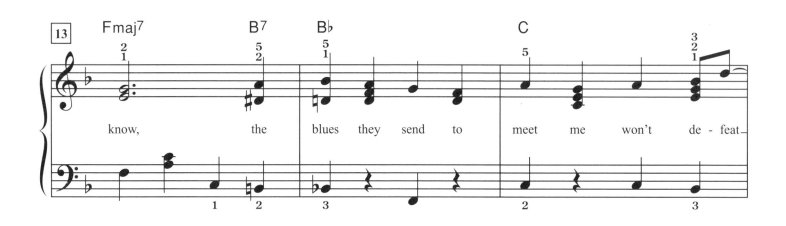

know,   the   blues they send to   meet   me   won't   de - feat

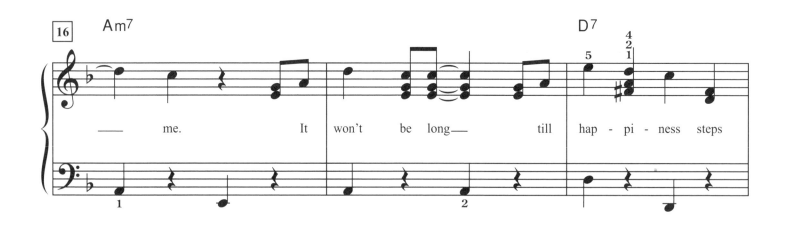

——   me.   It   won't   be   long——   till   hap - pi - ness   steps

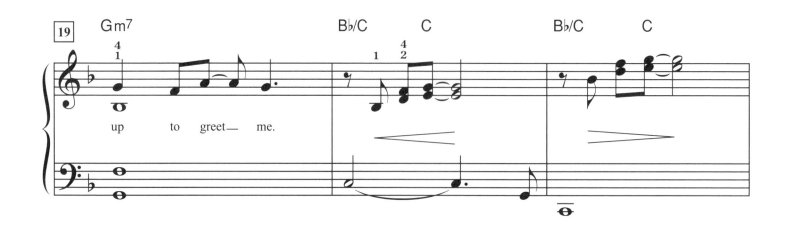

up   to   greet——   me.

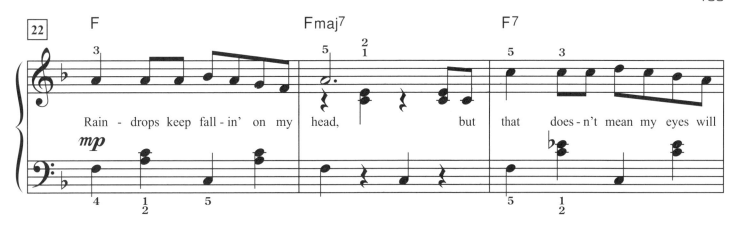

22

F   Fmaj7   F7

mp

Rain - drops keep fall - in' on my head,   but that does - n't mean my eyes will

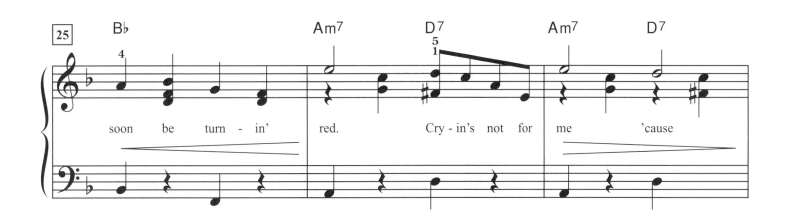

25

B♭   Am7   D7   Am7   D7

soon be turn - in' red.   Cry - in's not for me   'cause

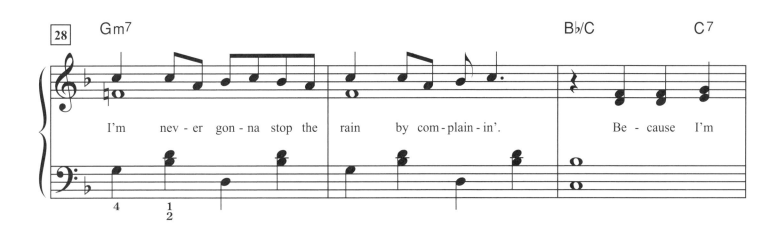

28

Gm7   B♭/C   C7

I'm nev - er gon - na stop the rain by com - plain - in'.   Be - cause I'm

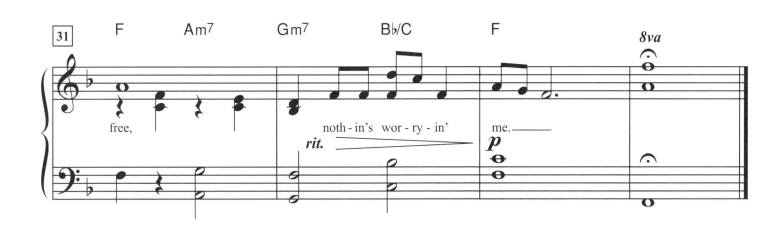

31

F   Am7   Gm7   B♭/C   F   *8va*

free,   noth - in's wor - ry - in' me.

rit.   *p*

RUNAROUND SUE

Rock and Roll Hall of Fame inductee Dion (DiMucci) recorded the Billboard chart-topping "Runaround Sue" with The Del-Satins in 1961. Before pursuing a solo career and recording with The Del-Satins, Dion sang with The Belmonts. Some of their biggest hits included "I Wonder Why," "A Teenager in Love," and "Where or When." In 1959, they toured with The Big Bopper, Buddy Holly, and Richie Valens—all of whom died during the tour in a plane crash. Dion had been offered a seat on the same plane but declined the offer.

Words and Music by
Dion DiMucci and Ernest Maresca
Arranged by Dan Coates

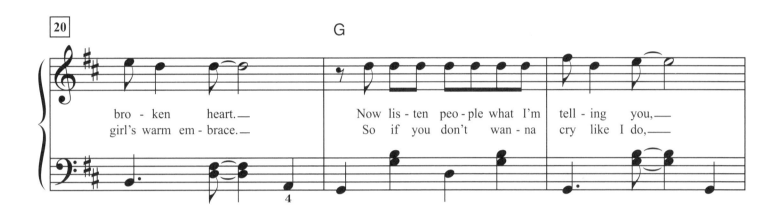

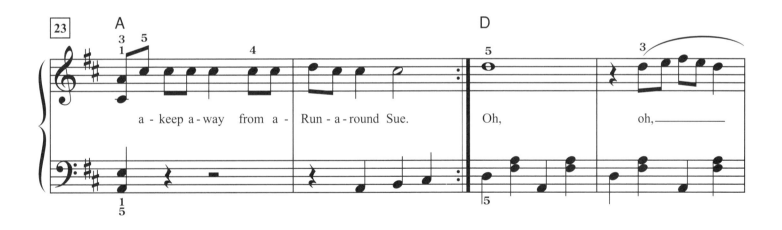

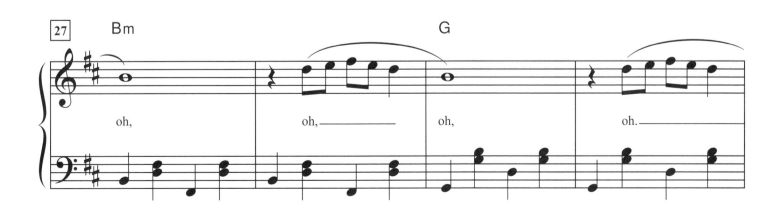

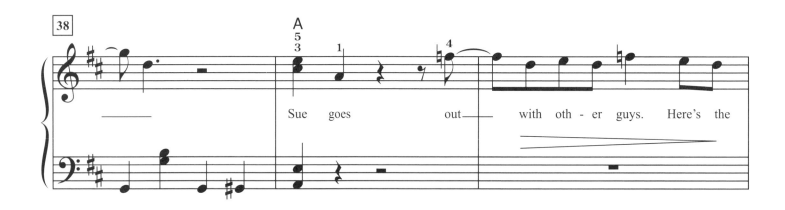

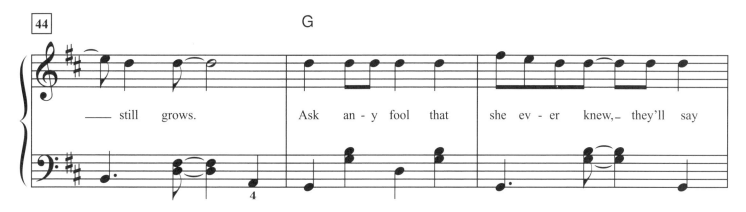

still grows. Ask an-y fool that she ev-er knew,— they'll say

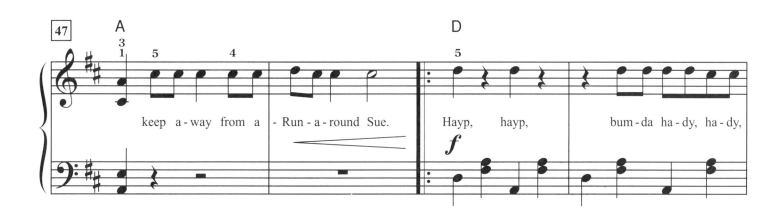

keep a-way from a - Run-a-round Sue. Hayp, hayp, bum-da ha-dy, ha-dy,

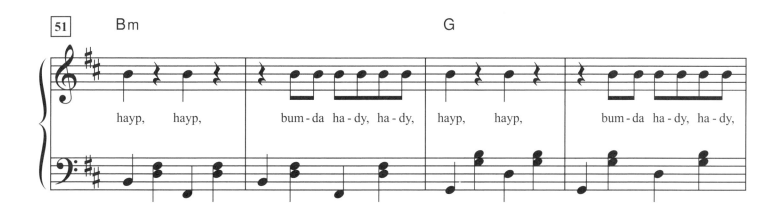

hayp, hayp, bum-da ha-dy, ha-dy, hayp, hayp, bum-da ha-dy, ha-dy,

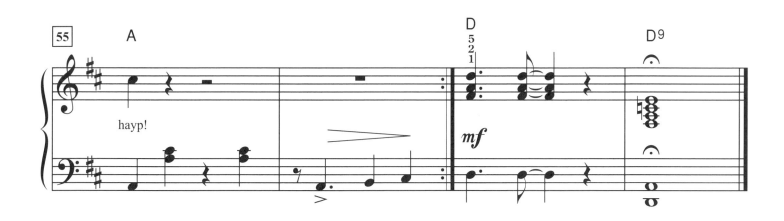

hayp!

SAVE THE LAST DANCE FOR ME

Ben E. King and The Drifters brought "Save the Last Dance for Me" to #1 on the U.S. pop charts in 1960. It has been notably recorded by Ike and Tina Turner, Emmylou Harris and Dolly Parton, Harry Nilsson (produced by John Lennon), and Michael Bublé.

Words by Doc Pomus
Music by Mort Shuman
Arranged by Dan Coates

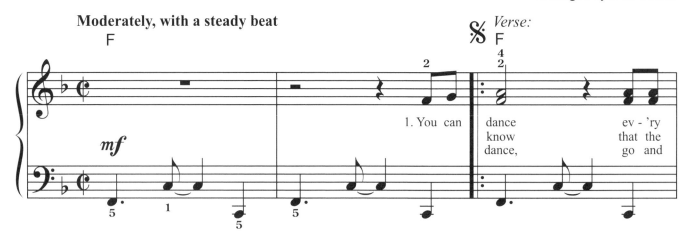

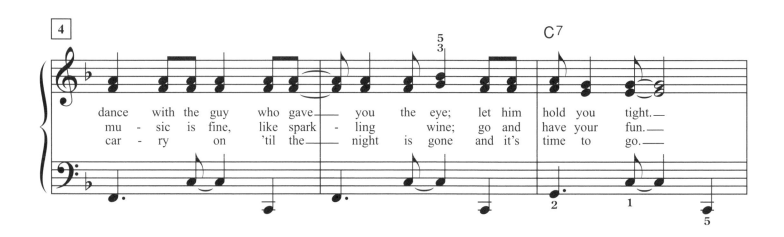

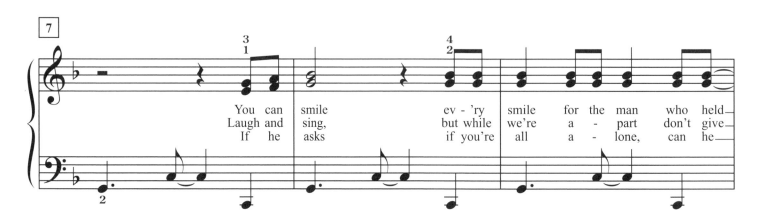

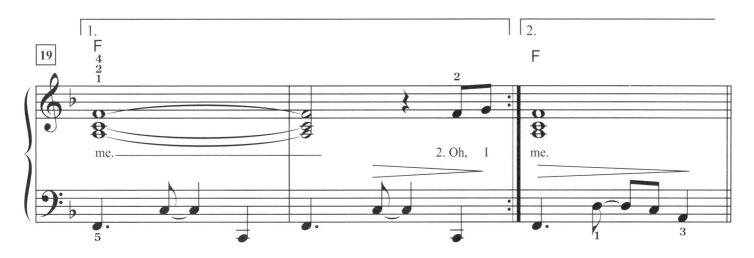

SEALED WITH A KISS

"Sealed with a Kiss" was first recorded in 1960 by The Four Voices. Brian Hyland released it as a single in 1962, and it reached #3 on both the Billboard Hot 100 and the UK Singles Chart. A number of other artists have covered the song including: Gary Lewis and the Playboys, Jason Donovan, The Letterman, Bobby Vee, The Shadows, and others. It has also been performed in French under the title "Derniers baisers (Last Kiss)" by Laurent Voulzy, and also by Les chats sauvages with singer Mike Shannon.

Music by Gary Geld
Words by Peter Udell
Arranged by Dan Coates

114

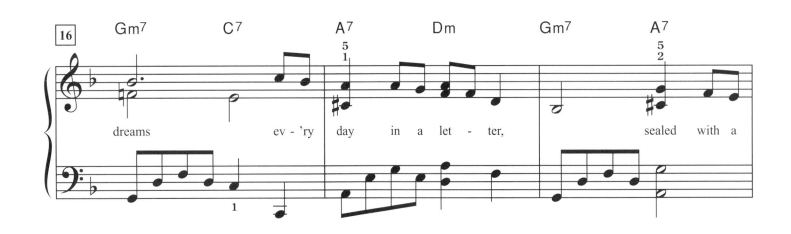

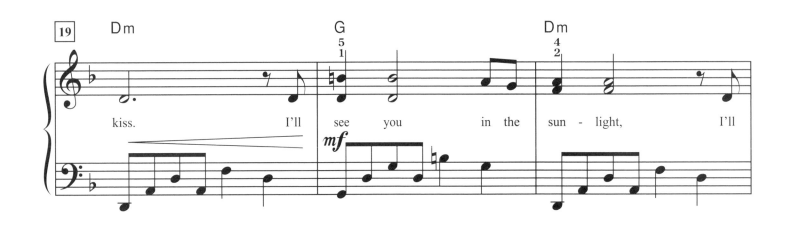

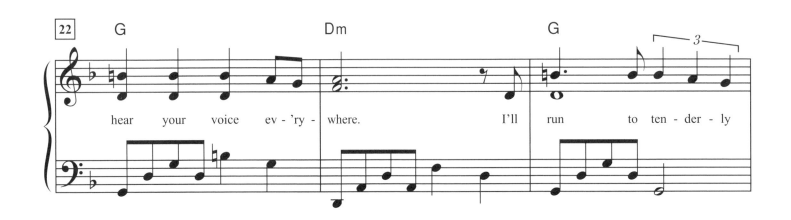

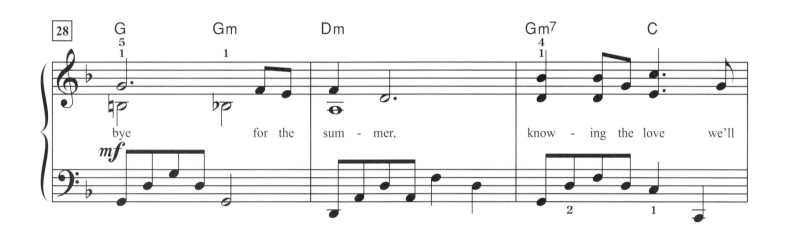

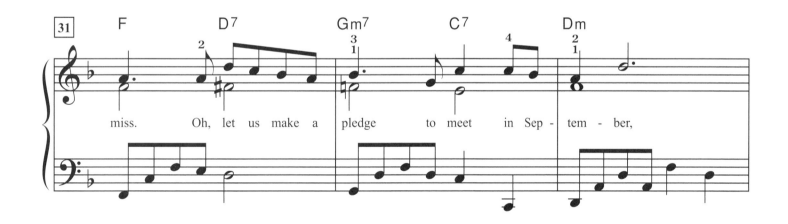

THE SHADOW OF YOUR SMILE

In 1965 Vincente Minnelli directed Richard Burton and Elizabeth Taylor in *The Sandpiper*, a story about a single mother who has a romance with the headmaster of a boarding school. Their love theme, "The Shadow of Your Smile," won the Academy Award for Best Original Song. Since then, it has been performed and recorded by many singing legends: Tony Bennett, Barbra Streisand, Perry Como, and Frank Sinatra, to name a few.

Music by Johnny Mandel
Lyric by Paul Francis Webster
Arranged by Dan Coates

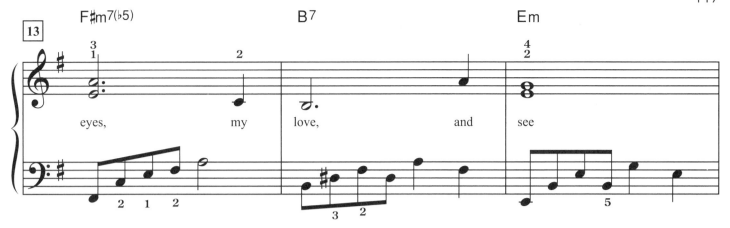

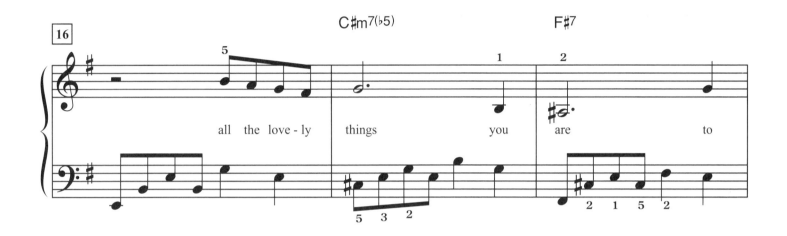

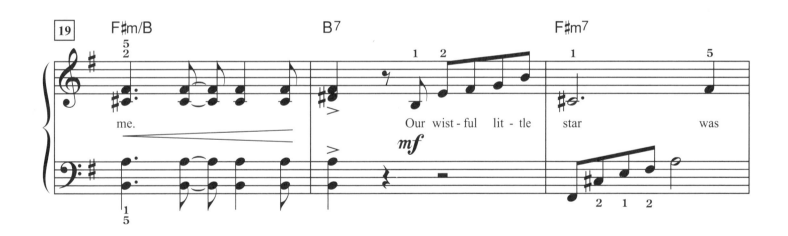

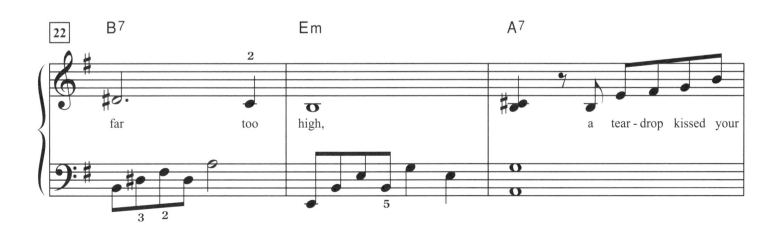

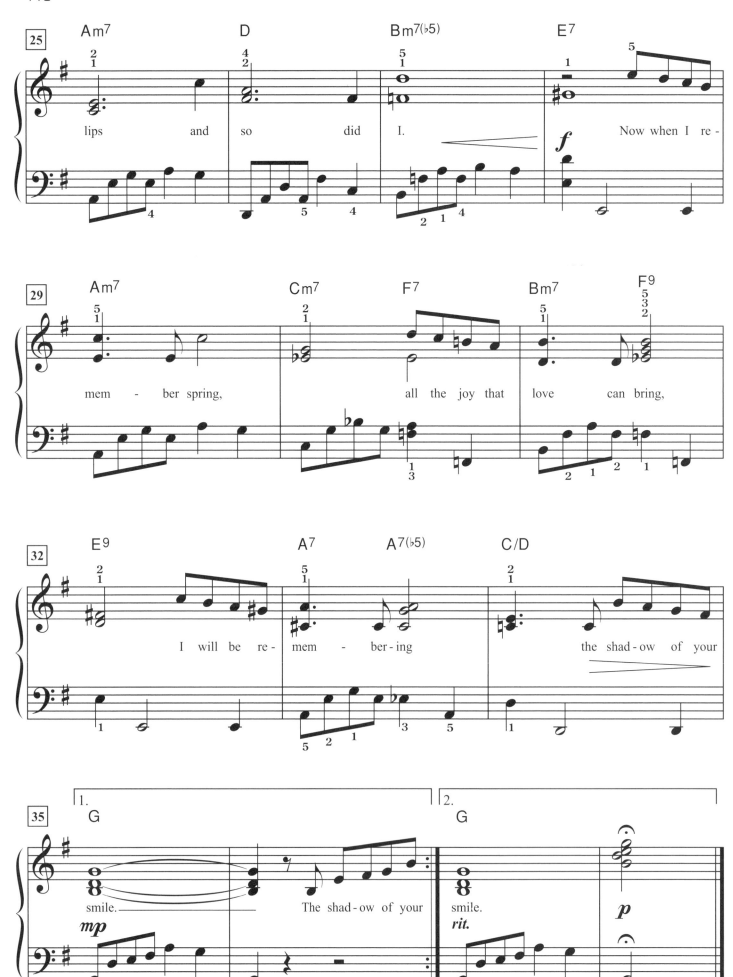

THIS MAGIC MOMENT

"This Magic Moment" was originally released by Ben E. King and The Drifters in 1960. It is similar in style to their other mega hit, "Stand by Me," which also uses King's melancholy voice over the common '50s chord progression (I vi IV V). In 1969, Jay & The Americans covered the song earning gold record status.

Words and Music by
Doc Pomus and Mort Shuman
Arranged by Dan Coates

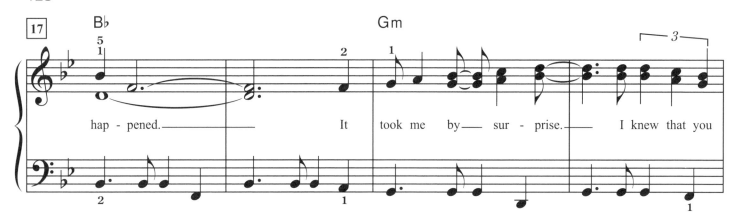

17 B♭   Gm

hap - pened.— It took me by— sur - prise.— I knew that you

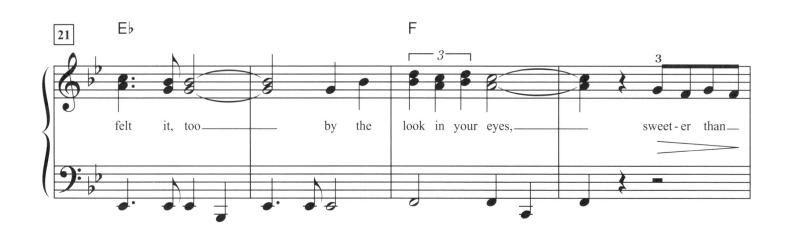

21 E♭   F

felt it, too— by the look in your eyes,— sweet - er than—

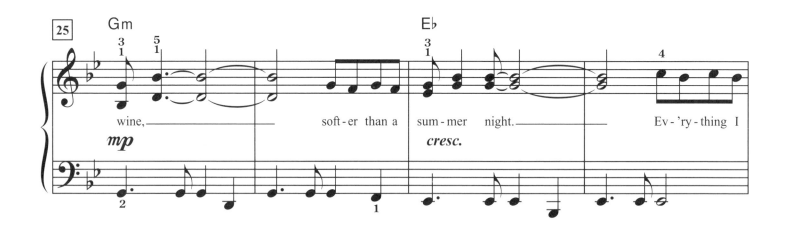

25 Gm   E♭

wine,— soft - er than a sum - mer night.— Ev - 'ry - thing I

mp   *cresc.*

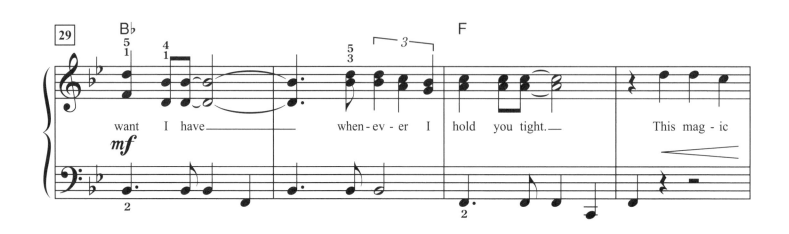

29 B♭   F

want I have— when - ev - er I hold you tight.— This mag - ic

mf

SOMEWHERE MY LOVE

Doctor Zhivago (published in 1957) is an epic novel set against the backdrop of the 1917 Russian Revolution. In 1965, it was made into an award-winning film, directed by David Lean, starring Omar Sharif (Yuri Zhivago) and Julie Christie (Larissa "Lara" Antipova). Maurice Jarre composed the music for the film which became popular worldwide. The music that accompanied Lara's scenes, "Lara's Theme," was particularly well-received, and in 1966 Ray Conniff added lyrics to the music and recorded it with his Ray Conniff Singers, entitling it "Somewhere My Love."

Music by Maurice Jarre
Lyric by Paul Francis Webster
Arranged by Dan Coates

Moderately, with expression

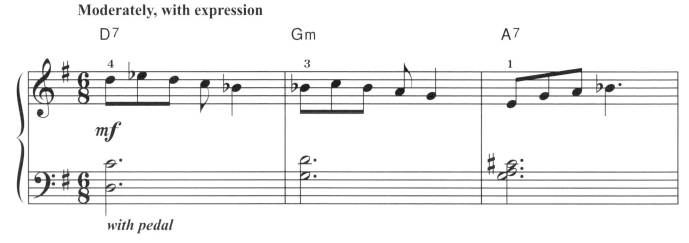

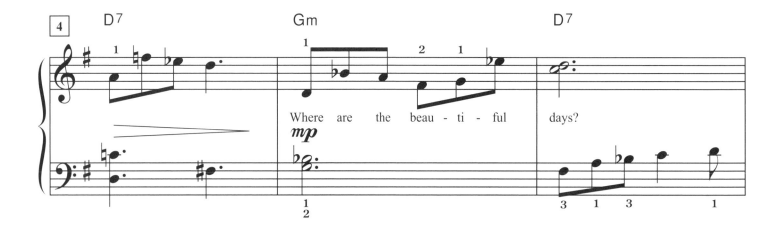

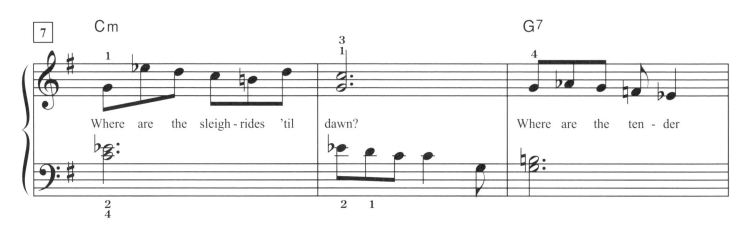

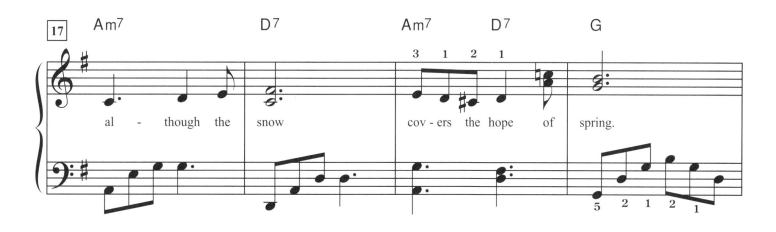

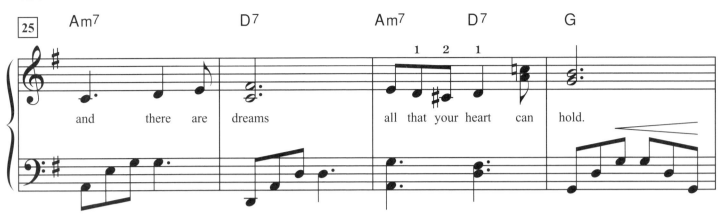

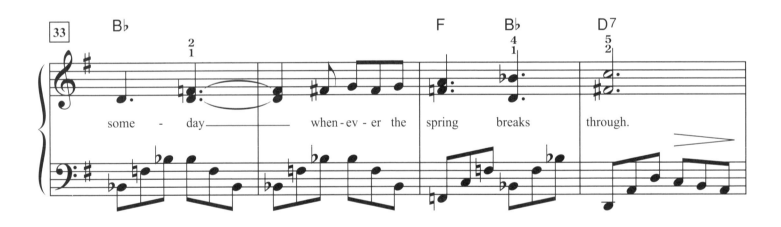

TURN! TURN! TURN!
(TO EVERYTHING THERE IS A SEASON)

"I swear it's not too late" is the only part of the lyric of "Turn! Turn! Turn!" written by its composer, Pete Seeger. The rest of the words come from the Ecclesiastes chapter of the King James version of the Bible, text that is often interpreted as a call for peace. When the folk-rock band The Byrds covered the song in October of 1965, just months after the beginning of the Vietnam War, it quickly climbed to the top of the charts and became one of the most important songs of the era.

Words from the Book of Ecclesiastes
Adaptation and Music by Pete Seeger

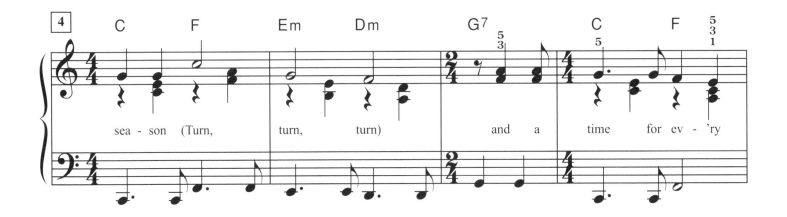

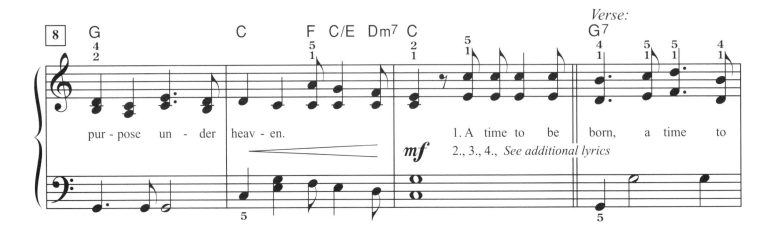

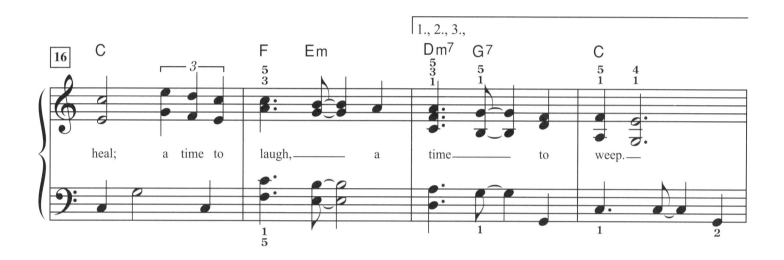

Verse 2:
A time to build up, a time to break down;
A time to dance, a time to mourn;
A time to cast away stones;
A time to gather stones together.

Verse 3:
A time of love, a time of hate;
A time of war, a time of peace;
A time you may embrace;
A time to refrain from embracing.

Verse 4:
A time to gain, a time to lose;
A time to rend, a time to sew;
A time to love, a time to hate;
A time for peace, I swear it's not too late.

WHAT ARE YOU DOING THE REST OF YOUR LIFE?

Frank Sinatra, Barbra Streisand, Bill Evans, Johnny Mathis, and Julie Andrews have all worked magic with "What Are You Doing the Rest of Your Life?". The song was written for the 1969 film *Happy Ending* and was nominated for an Academy Award for Best Original Song. It won two Grammy Awards—in 1973 (as performed by Sarah Vaughan) and in 2006 (as performed by Chris Botti and Sting).

Lyrics by Alan and Marilyn Bergman
Music by Michel Legrand
Arranged by Dan Coates

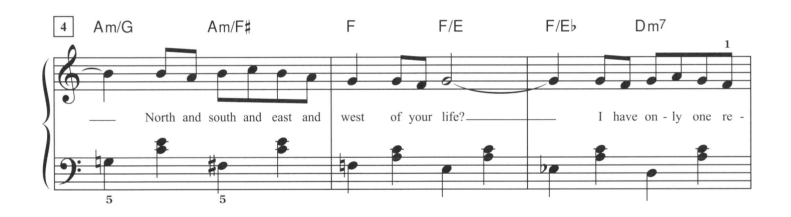

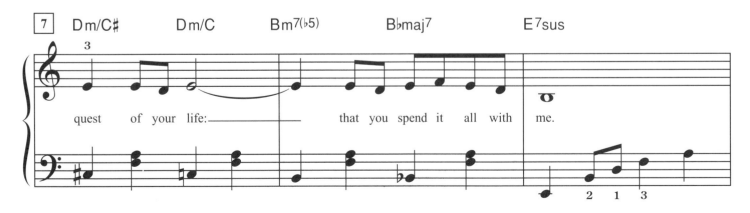

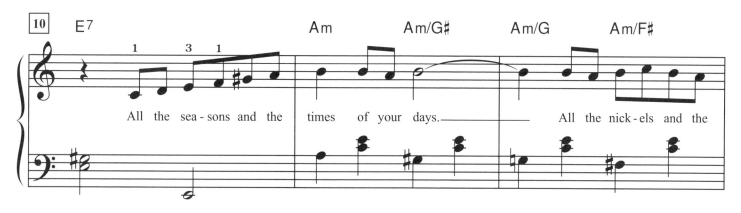

All the sea-sons and the times of your days._____ All the nick-els and the

dimes of your days._____ Let the rea-sons and the rhymes of your days_____

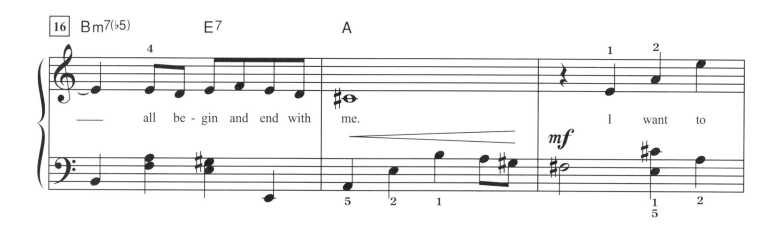

_____ all be-gin and end with me. I want to

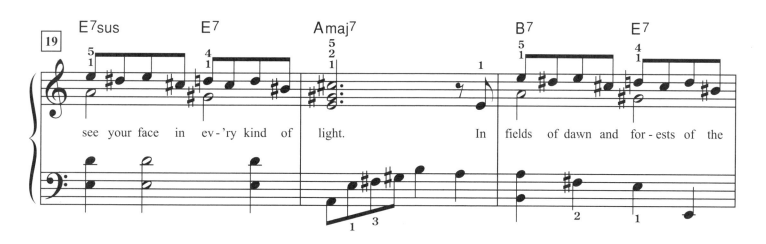

see your face in ev-'ry kind of light. In fields of dawn and for-ests of the

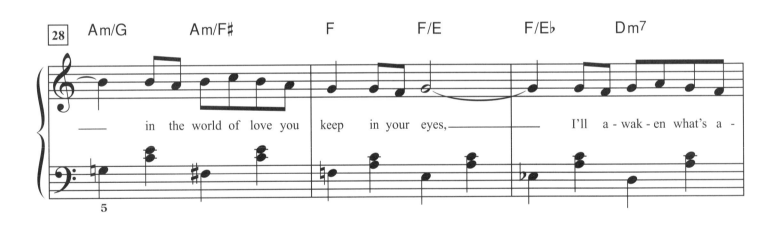

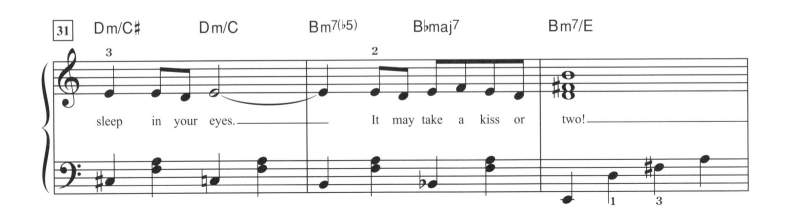

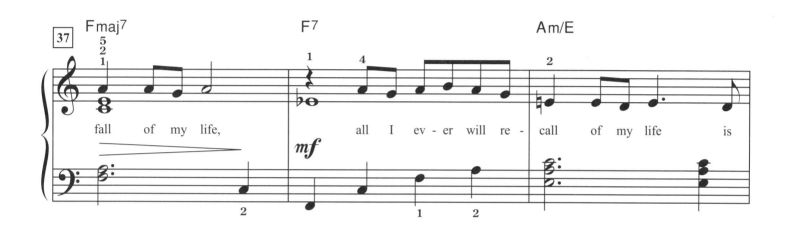

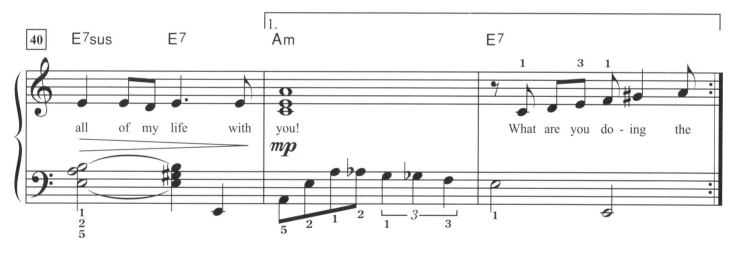

WHEN A MAN LOVES A WOMAN

Rock and Roll Hall of Fame inductee Percy Sledge recorded "When a Man Loves a Woman" in 1966. It quickly soared to the top of the charts and became the first gold record release for Atlantic Records. Michael Bolton covered the song in 1991, a single that earned him a Grammy Award.

Words and Music by
Calvin Lewis and Andrew Wright
Arranged by Dan Coates

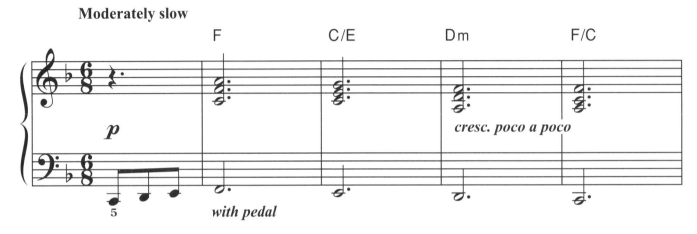

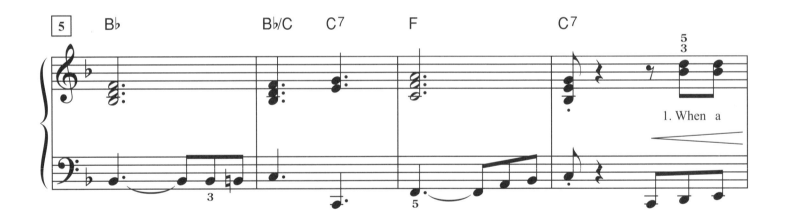

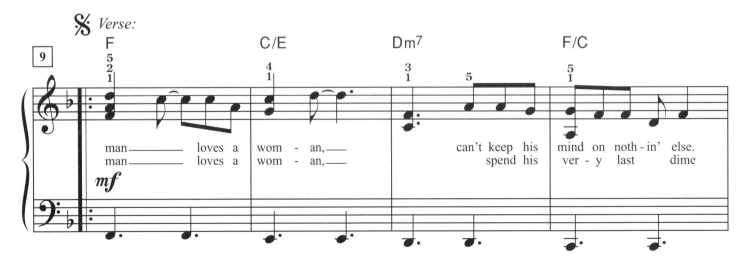

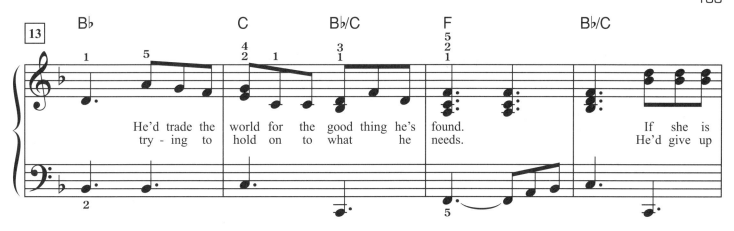

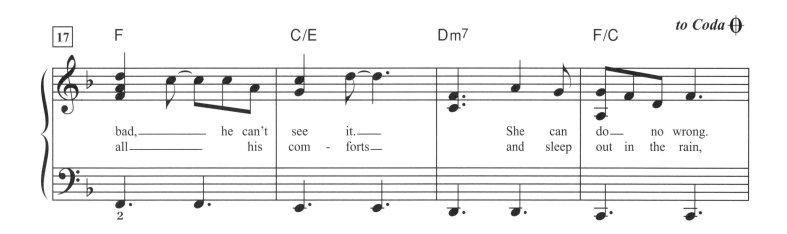

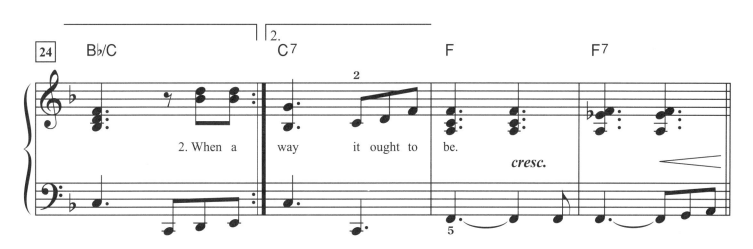

Bridge:

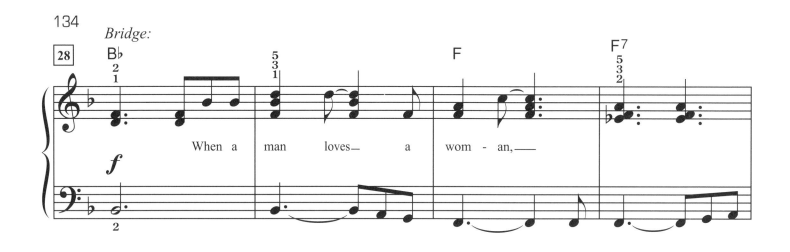

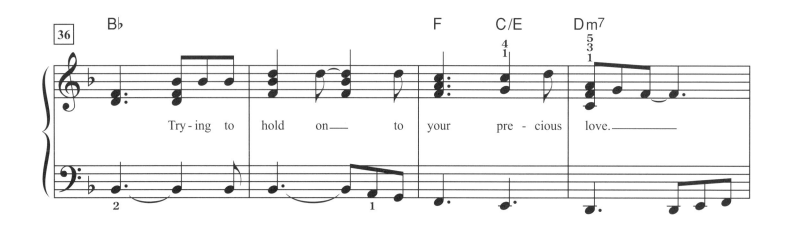

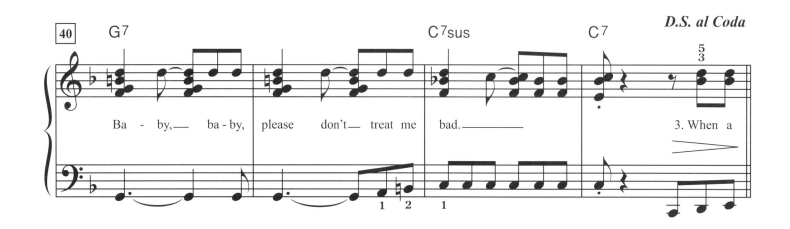

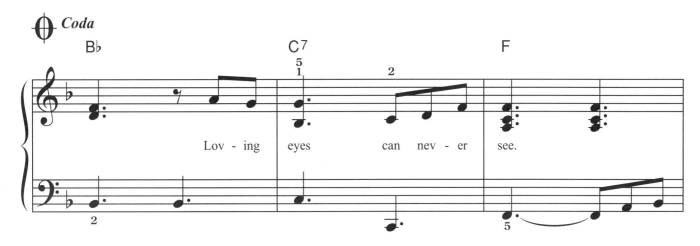

Coda

Lov - ing   eyes   can   nev - er   see.

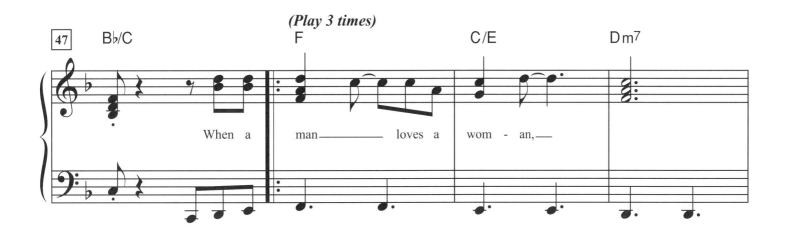

(Play 3 times)

When a   man——— loves a   wom - an,———

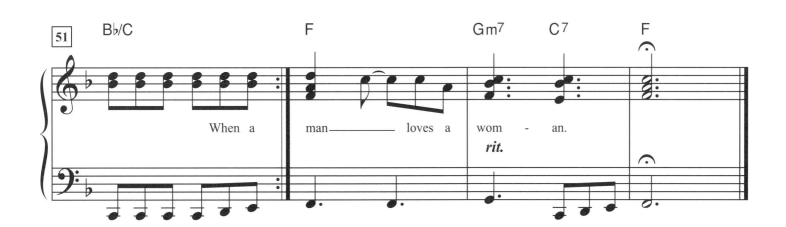

When a   man——— loves a   wom - an.

rit.

Verse 3:
When a man loves a woman,
Deep down in his soul,
She can bring him such misery.
If she is playing him for a fool,
He's the last one to know.
Loving eyes can never see.

THE WINDMILLS OF YOUR MIND

Oscar-, Grammy-, and Emmy-winning Michel Legrand wrote "The Windmills of Your Mind" for the 1968 film *The Thomas Crown Affair*, starring Steve McQueen and Faye Dunaway. The movie is modeled after the life of a Belgian art thief. It received the Academy Award that year for Best Original Song.

Lyrics by Marilyn and Alan Bergman
Music by Michel Legrand
Arranged by Dan Coates

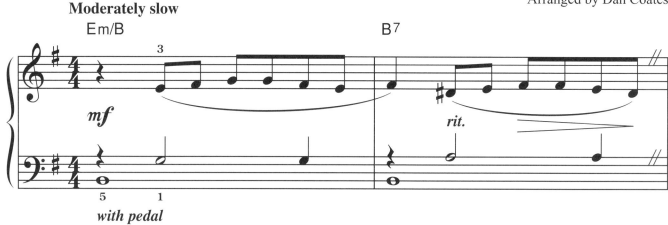

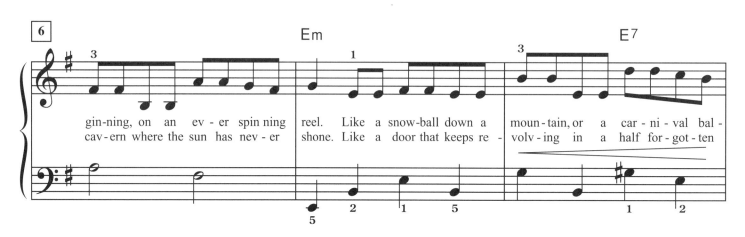

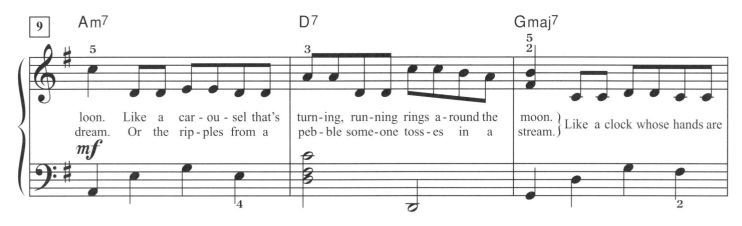

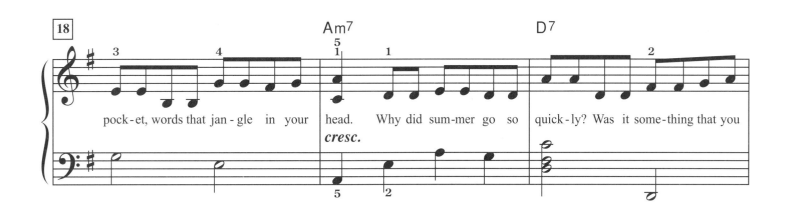

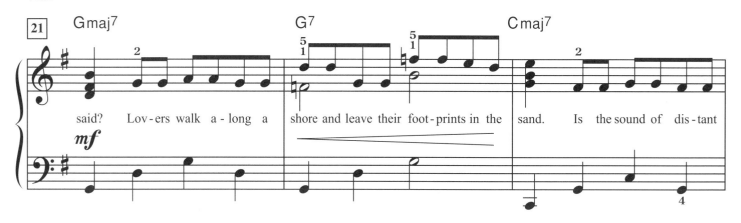

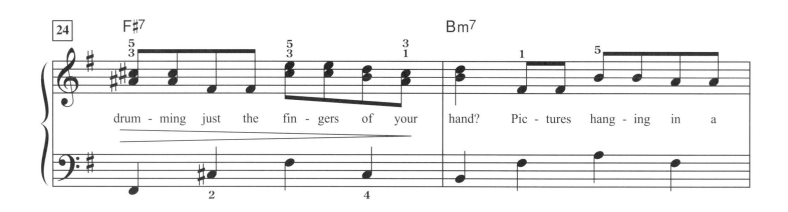

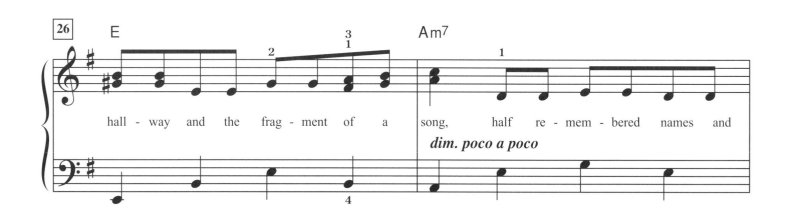

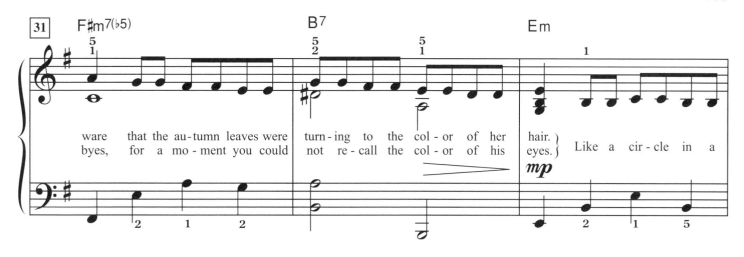

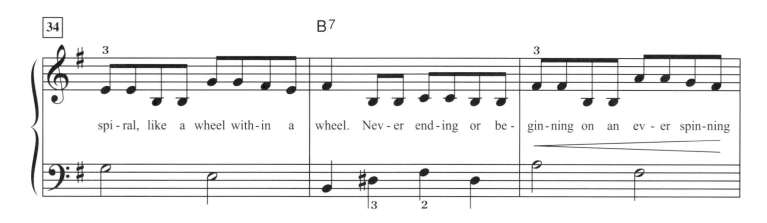

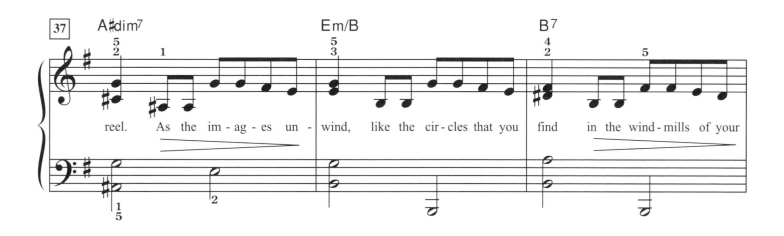

YOU'RE MY WORLD

Between 1964 and 1967 many rock and pop groups from England came to the United States. This is commonly known as the "British Invasion" and included such big names as The Beatles, The Who, and The Rolling Stones. Amidst all of this, British pop singer Cilla Black (from Liverpool, like The Beatles) emerged as well. She recorded "You're My World" in 1964.

Words and Music by Umberto Bindi and Gino Paoli
English Lyric by Carl Sigman
Arranged by Dan Coates

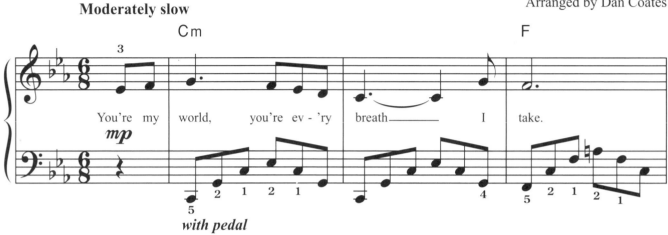

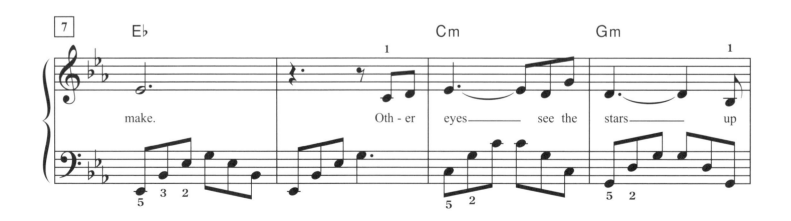

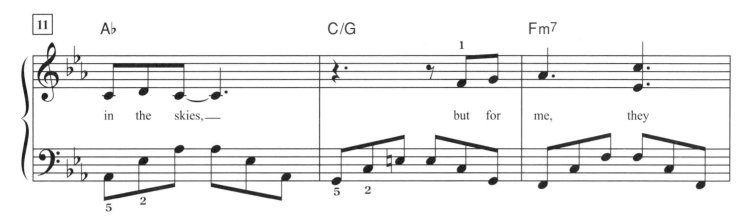

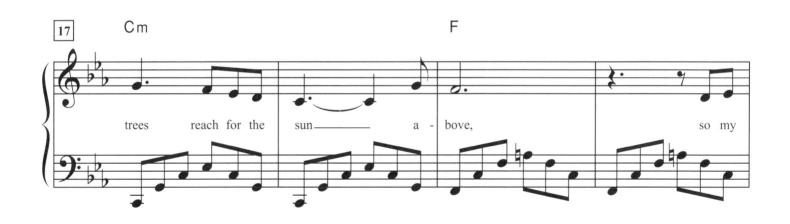

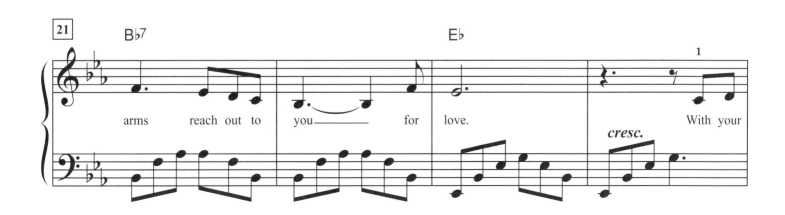

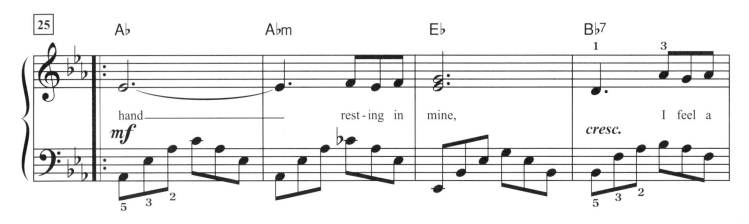

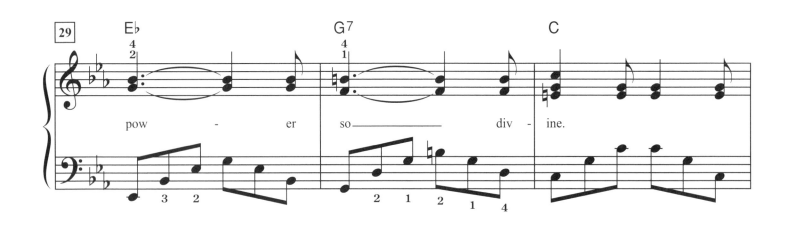

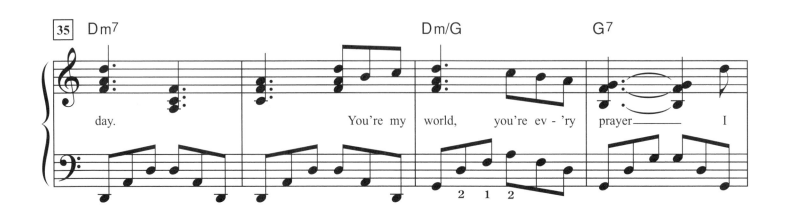